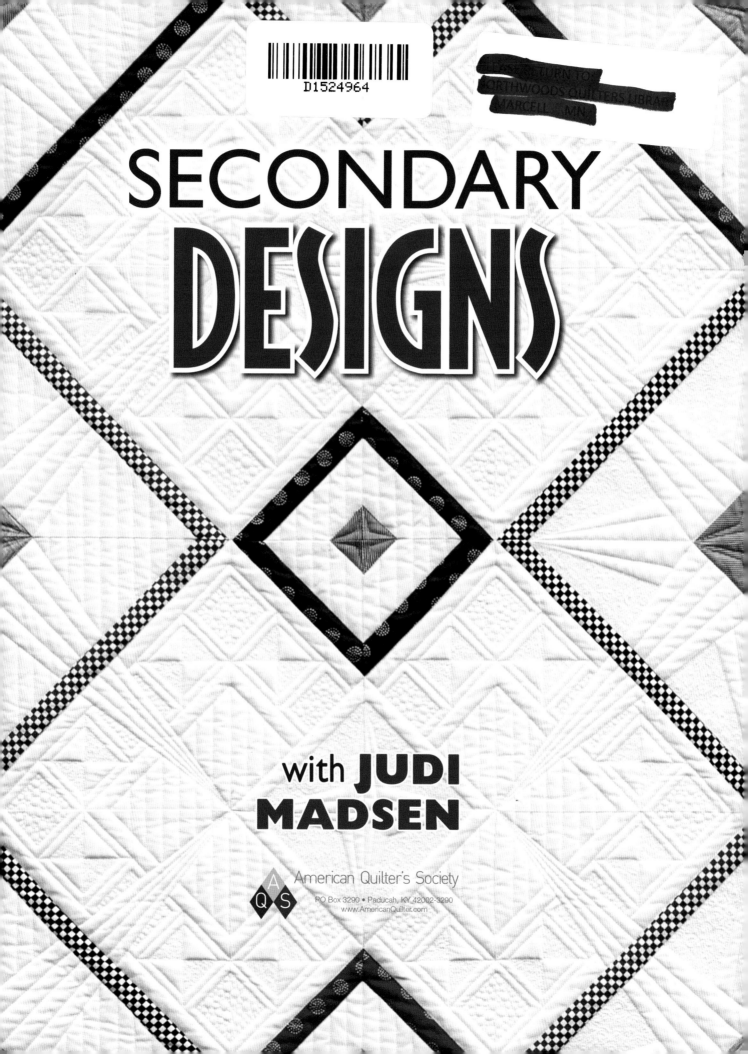

SECONDARY DESIGNS

with JUDI MADSEN

American Quilter's Society

PO Box 3290 • Paducah, KY 42002-3290
www.AmericanQuilter.com

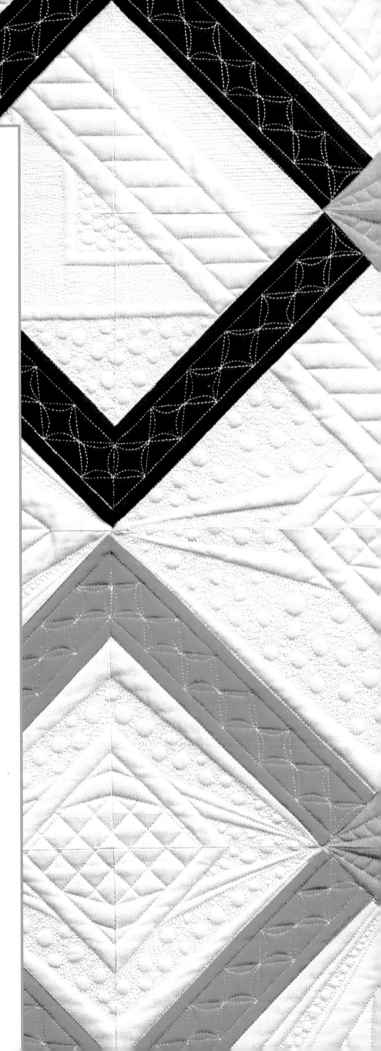

The American Quilter's Society or AQS is dedicated to quilting excellence. AQS promotes the triumphs of today's quilter, while remaining dedicated to the quilting tradition. We believe in the promotion of this art and craft through AQS Publishing and AQS QuiltWeek®.

CONTENT EDITOR: CAITLIN RIDINGS
COPY EDITOR: CHRYSTAL ABHALTER
GRAPHIC DESIGN: ELAINE WILSON
COVER DESIGN: SARAH BOZONE
PHOTOGRAPHY: CHARLES R. LYNCH, UNLESS OTHERWISE NOTED
ASSISTANT EDITOR: ADRIANA FITCH
DIRECTOR OF PUBLICATIONS: KIMBERLY HOLLAND TETREV

Additional copies of this book may be ordered from the American Quilter's Society, PO Box 3290, Paducah, KY 42002-3290, or online at www.ShopAQS.com.

Attention Photocopying Service: Please note the following—Publisher and author give permission to print images on the CD.

American Quilter's Society

www.AmericanQuilter.com

Library of Congress Cataloging-in-Publication Data

Names: Madsen, Judi, author.
Title: Secondary designs / with Judi Madsen.
Description: Paducah, KY : American Quilter's Society,, [2016]
Identifiers: LCCN 2016052070 | ISBN 9781683390091 (pbk.)
Subjects: LCSH: Quilting--Patterns.
Classification: LCC TT835 .M27129 2016 | DDC 746.46--dc23
LC record available at https://lccn.loc.gov/2016052070

COVER AND TITLE PAGE: NORTH STAR, full quilt, p. 76.
RIGHT: DIAMOND IN THE ROUGH, full quilt, p. 29.

Dedication

We did it! We survived another book! This one goes out to my husband and best friend, Clint, and our four amazing children who get the brunt of my stress from creating under pressure. I cannot imagine life without you! Thank you so much for supporting me, encouraging me, and making me dinner almost every night during crunch time! I love you!

For my mom and sisters who keep me laughing and keep me humble, you put up with my endless texts of sneak peeks and are the first to see my projects, I live for your approval. Thank you for loving this crazy sister and daughter of yours. Love you!

To my Savior, the more I create the closer I feel to you. I hope that I am worthy of the love and patience you have shown me. I pray that I will be more like you. Thank you for the gift of quilting—it has forever changed my life for the better.

PHOTO CREDIT: Amber Wallis of Carly Grace Photography

Acknowledgments

Thank you to Hobbs Batting for your amazing batting that I love! The new cotton/wool blend is my favorite!

Thank you Superior Threads for creating So Fine! and Kimono Silk thread. I love them both.

Thank you Fil-Tec Bobbin Central for making Glide thread and Magna-Glide bobbins. I love you. I do not have to wind my own anymore.

Thank you Moda Fabrics for making Moda Bella Solids. I went through several bolts of the bleached white cotton as well as countless other colors and prints I pulled from my stash to make the projects in this book. I could not make amazing quilts without fabulous fabric, so thank you!

A huge thank you goes to Thelma Childers.

You are quite possibly the best piecer out there. Thank you so much for piecing STAR X-ING and PLAYTIME for me. You saved me on time that I desperately needed. Thank you so much!

Thank you Meredith Schroeder and Lynn Loyd for making me feel like part of the AQS family. Thanks for saying yes to publishing my second book! I am so grateful to you!

Thank you to Kim Tetrev, Elaine Brelsford, Ginny Borgia, and for all the staff at AQS Publishing who have worked with me on this book. Your editing skills are amazing! Thank you for making this book as beautiful as I envisioned it to be.

To You – you have purchased my books, attended my classes, followed my blog, and followed me on social media. I would not be where I am today without you. Thank you!

Contents

ON THE CD
HERE IS A LOOK INTO
MY CREATIVE SPACE

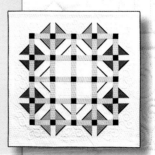

OPPOSITE AND RIGHT: BIG BERTHA, full quilt, p. 57

Introduction

2006

2009

Here we go again! I cannot believe that I am writing another quilting book. My first book was a goal I set for myself that seemed unreachable at times. The reality of writing two books never entered my mind when I started quilting over 11 years ago. My first book, *Quilting Wide Open Spaces,* was fun to write, and I am so proud of it—I always will be. But this second book is the icing on the cake for me. I look at the quilting in my first book and compare it to the quilting in this book and cry at the difference. Practice, as they say, makes perfect (or it makes for consistency, because no one is perfect and I am far from that). I am so happy with how my quilting has progressed through the years. So, look at your quilting and try to improve, but make sure you are comparing your quilting to your own quilting and do not compare it to others because as Theodore Roosevelt said, *"Comparison is the thief of joy."* Your goal should be to improve your quilting skills. By comparing your quilting through the years, the obvious improvement should help in giving you a boost of confidence.

Here is a look at my quilting through the years.

In the first picture, you can see that I was a beginner, big time. This was one of my first "custom" quilted quilts. I quilted an orange peel design that was completely free motion and you can tell by the different sizes of each shape that I did not have any real control of my machine. At this point in my quilting journey, I was confident and excited to custom quilt. Seriously, if I quilted like that now, I would have more time to piece quilt tops—my first love!

The second picture shows my small quilting that was fun, but not awesome. This quilt was a humbling quilt for me. I was so proud of it because it took me so long to quilt. The small "pebble" quilting looks more like loops on crack. Just because the quilting is small doesn't mean it looks good. I entered this quilt into a show and expected to win an award. When it did not win, I threw a fit! How could a quilt that I spent so much time on not win an award? Well, thanks to my mom, she brought me back down to earth. With her reasoning and good judgment, she told me how immature I was being. I can now look at that quilt and be grateful for the lesson it taught me. First, don't become so confident that you look and act like a snob. Second, don't expect to win an award, but be gracious and excited when you do. I still have to remind myself that from time to time.

The third quilting picture shows my quilting from my *Quilting Wide Open Spaces* book. I love the quilting. I think it looks great, but I want to show you the difference between the third and fourth picture with the filler designs. The pebbling is so much more precise in the fourth picture. The quilting I did in these pictures are three years apart. You can see how the years of practice have helped me to improve.

I hope that by showing you my comparisons, you can take a moment to pat yourself on the back because your quilting has improved. Do not get discouraged, don't compare your quilting to others, and keep practicing. You will accomplish your quilting goals if you just work hard enough.

I have been quilting in a secondary design style for a few years now, so it was an obvious fit when I came up with the concept for my second book. I love being able to look at a quilt top and see the potential quilting designs that can be created in the background. The background is where I want to shine as a quilter. I want to create quilting designs that take my breath away and designs that give me the satisfaction of creating something out of nothing. There is something to be said about creating. It

2011

2014

gives you self-confidence like nothing else could. To make something out of nothing is why I create. I love the feeling I get from it, and I am sure you do too.

"God left the world unfinished for man to work his skill upon. He left the electricity in the cloud, the oil in the earth. He left the rivers unbridged and the forests uncut, and the cities unbuilt. God gives to man the challenge of raw materials, not the ease and comfort of finished things. He leaves the pictures unpainted and the music unsung and the problems unsolved, that man might know the joys and glories of creation." Thomas S. Monson

The projects in this book have the instructions on how to piece the quilt top and how to quilt each section of the secondary quilting design. I hope that as I walk you through each project, you can get a chance to understand my design style and my thought process for coming up with secondary quilting designs. The possibilities are endless when it comes to design, and I hope that you feel encouraged to push the limits of quilting, because as artists, we all benefit with raising the bar.

So, enjoy the journey, improve your skills, but don't take yourself too seriously. Nobody likes a stick in the mud.

Judi

OPPOSITE: NORTH STAR, back detail, full quilt, p. 76.

Secondary Designs

Each pieced quilt has endless possibilities of secondary quilting designs. You just have to take a minute or several days to look at your quilt top and the empty spaces to see what design possibilities there are. I don't always plan out all of my quilting designs when I design a quilt top, and more than likely I will change my quilting design plans as the quilt top speaks to me. However, my latest designs have purposely had more empty spaces so that I can focus on the quilting designs. It is important to me that the quilting and piecing work well together, but I definitely like to shine in the quilting area. If you can come up with the right balance for quilting and piecing, then you have made it!

There are times that quilters mistake heavy detailed quilting as an appropriate quilting design. You should have a design plan, not a rigid one that cannot be unchanged, but a plan nonetheless. You should not just throw detailed quilting on a quilt and think that it will work every time. Believe me, I have seen some quilts that look like a "hot mess" of crazy texture. These quilting designs take away from the piecing design and because of the "detailed quilting movement" (which I am totally guilty of) there are a lot of customers now looking for more detailed quilting. In that same breath, they don't want to pay for the time it takes to quilt super detailed. Because of that, a lot of quilters have made the choice to quilt heavily, but quilting without a purpose and quilting mostly large detailed free-motion designs. It is like they are quilting a tight allover design and calling it a custom quilting job. Don't get me wrong, if your customer is happy, then by all means do it. I think it is so important to have a plan and purpose for your custom quilting so that the design adds to the piecing and does not take away from the overall look of the quilt. Remember, just because you can quilt detailed shapes and designs does not mean the designs will work on every quilt.

Quilting secondary designs take time and lots of it. I am not going to sugar coat the concept of this quilt book and tell you that you will finish these projects fast, because most likely you will not. All of my designs are meant to push the limits of quilting, and hopefully take me and you to the next level. I believe anyone can quilt the way that I do if they just have the patience to do it. I don't feel like the quilting I do is particularly hard. It is just monotonous to the point of sheer boredom. Serious. There are times when I cannot quilt one more stitch, but for some crazy reason I always finish a project. The reason I do is because the payoff is so rewarding. When I pull a quilt off the frames, I am flooded with tears of joy, seriously! The time it took me to quilt, all the hard work, the broken back, and free time I did not have suddenly don't matter anymore because the quilt I just finished is beautiful! It's gorgeous! I cannot wait to take pictures and share it with all of you! I can't wait to hold the quilt in the sunlight to see all the beautiful texture; it is just so rewarding. I hope that you feel that same excitement as you take the time to quilt the projects in this book.

You will need three essential tools in this book to complete the secondary quilting designs: a straight ruler, a marking pen, and a quilting machine. I use purple disappearing markers almost exclusively for marking my quilts, and I used a lot of markers for the projects in this book. Plan on using anywhere from 2 to 3 disappearing markers per quilt top. The straight-edge ruler I received when I purchased my A1 longarm machine is my favorite quilting tool.

This 9" ruler has etched lines to help me with marking, and the handle is so helpful for keeping my quilting lines as straight as possible (fig. 1). I use this ruler to mark a lot of the design lines in this book, but the larger design lines will require a larger ruler.

Fig. 1. 9" ruler

I use my large rotary-cutting rulers when I have lines that need to be marked before I put the quilt on the frames. When the lines are longer than 9", I use the blue water-soluble marker for lines that need to be marked before I put the quilt on the frames. To get the lines out, I use a spray bottle of water to spritz on the lines and an extra piece of batting to rub out marks. Let the marks completely disappear by air drying before you advance your quilt.

Now that you are aware that you only need a few tools and a whole lot of patience, it's time to talk about the projects in this book. I hope to show you a little of how the lines within each project helped me come up with the secondary quilting designs.

The Designs!

DIAMOND IN THE ROUGH

This design is a great example of using the whole pieced top as the background for the secondary design (fig. 2). When you look at the quilting compared to the piecing, the lines created from the seam allowances are lost, and you can no longer determine where each block is. You can see in the completed project how your eyes are no longer looking at the seams in the pieced design but are instead drawn to the secondary design. I used the piecing to come up with my designs by drawing lines from point to point with the grey background fabric.

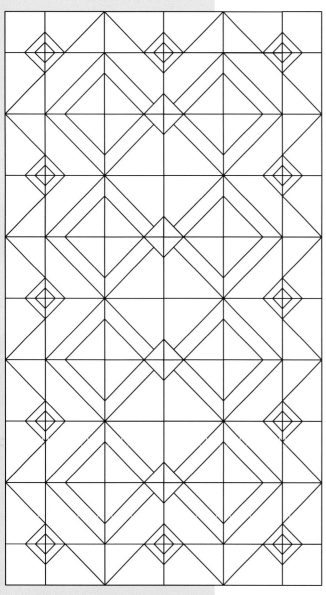

Fig. 2. DIAMOND IN THE ROUGH outline drawing

Fig. 3. DIAMOND IN THE ROUGH

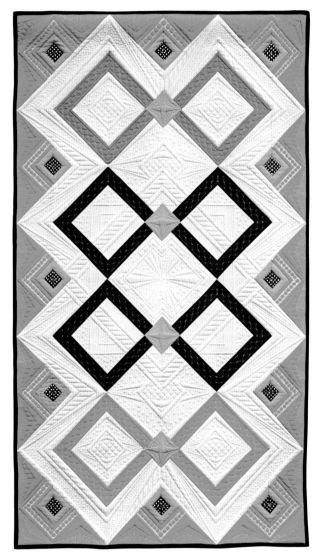

Fig. 4. DIAMOND IN THE ROUGH

The diamond shapes quilted in the grey fabric background (fig. 3) perfectly complement the diamond shapes in the piecing and give so much more to this quilt top (fig. 4). The secondary design makes this quilt top pop. It just wouldn't be the same quilt if the quilting were not as spectacular.

The quilting in this project looks pretty fantastic and almost flawless, but I want to share with you the mistakes in this quilt top—just to show you that I am human and that I have no desire to take out itty-bitty stitches. If you make a mistake on a quilt, then make the same mistake on the opposite side of the quilt, or just tweak the design a little to make it work for you. Here is how I fixed my mistakes on this quilt top (fig. 5, p. 14).

Fig. 5

1. The pieced green fabric on-point square was originally going to have the connecting curve stitches shown opposite at point #1, but when I quilted out the first square I did not like it. I thought the balance of quilting was off and that there was too much detail. The remaining green squares in the quilt are untouched and look a lot better. Why didn't I take out the stitching? I like to keep mistakes in a quilt to help remind me that I don't have to be perfect when it comes to quilting. It also helps me to learn from those mistakes by keeping the stitches in and serves as a reminder to not make the same mistake again. I know now with this quilt top that sometimes less is more and that having a balance between dense quilting and minimal quilting is important.

2. There is no mistake at point #2, but I show you this to let you know that this is how I originally designed this motif. It has three straight lines coming out from the top and bottom corners on both sides of the squares. In point #3 I forgot to draw the third line on each side, and you can see that it clearly was not quilted. I panicked a little after I noticed this. There was no way that I could take the stitching out with the scribble quilting I did. So, I made it work by first mimicking the mistake in the diamond below. I also quilted the correct design in the diamond below point #2. Now both sides of the designs look like I meant to do that, right?

3. The final fix for the mistake was to stitch the same mistake motif with the two lines on the opposite side of the middle of the quilt at point #4. Then, I quilted the original design with

three lines on the opposite side at point #5. I made my mistake make sense for the quilt, and it has a symmetrical feeling to it. So when it comes down to it, really there are no mistakes, so do not get discouraged.

Note: The instructions for the quilting design for DIAMOND IN THE ROUGH will not include the mistake. So your quilt will look better than mine.

STAR X-ING (fig. 6)

Fig. 6. STAR X-ING outline drawing

This design is an example of using the piecing as inspiration for the secondary design. The arrows within the border piecing design (fig. 6) gave me the idea for the arrows in the center rows of the quilt top (fig. 7).

The quilted arrows complement the piecing and give the quilt a secondary design. Also, the pieced square was treated as another secondary design by quilting it differently than the background and the arrows. You can see how using the shapes and piecing within the quilt will give plenty of ideas for secondary designs.

The background quilting with its on-point diamond filler mimics the on-point squares in the border designs and is also the inspiration for the on-point squares between the arrow designs.

The other rows of the quilt take the on-point square shape to another level by making it bigger and creating an incredible secondary design (fig. 8).

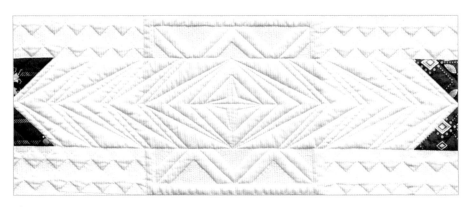

Fig. 7

Fig. 8

You can see how I use the same designs or quilting lines within a quilt top. I just change the size and location of those designs. The designs then work together to create a balanced and beautiful secondary design that complements the piecing.

One of the questions that I am asked all the time is, "Isn't the quilt stiff with all that detail?" I always answer that it is a little stiffer than quilts that don't have the detail. I am not necessarily going to be cuddling with this quilt that took me 90 hours to quilt. It is funny to me that the art of machine quilting is not appreciated totally yet—as if it isn't considered a quilt. Most of the quilts I have worked on have two layers of batting, and all of the quilts in this book have two layers of batting. The double layer of batting helps with the stiffness, especially when you use wool batting as one of the layers. Because I use my quilt tops for show and sharing, I haven't had the time to wash and dry my quilts. I don't see the need to do it. However, because I had trouble with my original STAR X-ING quilt, (explained in the project on the CD) I had the chance to wash the quilt with all that detail, and I can tell you the quilt is soft and amazing. I am sure I will use it as an everyday quilt once I am finished showing it. The picture shows how soft the fabric and quilting look after I washed my quilt (fig. 9).

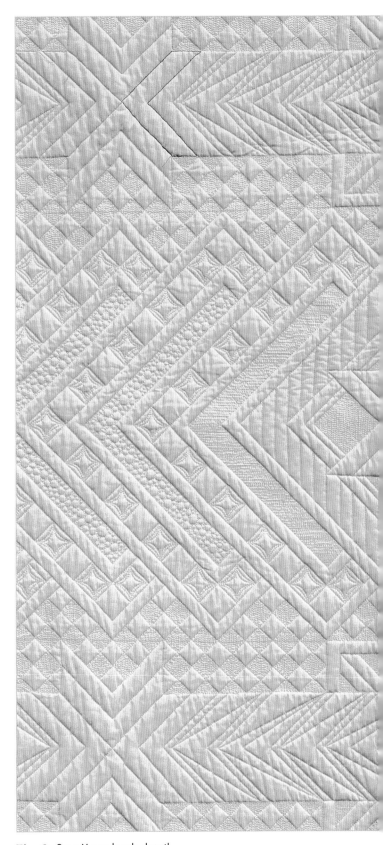

Fig. 9. STAR X-ING back detail

Fig. 10. BIG BERTHA outline drawing

Fig. 11. BIG BERTHA original drawing

BIG BERTHA

The horizontal and vertical piecing lines in this quilt are very simple, although a lot of times it can be difficult to design beyond those lines (fig. 10). When I first started quilting, I would have filled in the space with pretty standard quilting designs, probably feathers, and I would have let the horizontal and vertical lines shine. When you are planning to use a secondary design on a quilt you need to look beyond the lines of the quilt and see lines going in a different direction. One of the tools I use to help me come up with secondary designs is graph paper. The lines in the paper helped me with geometric designs, and I easily came up with different ways to quilt in the background.

The original drawing of BIG BERTHA was based on a 10" block and 4" sashing (fig. 11). The quilting design is the one I planned on using when I chose projects for this book, but I realized that this particular design would be more difficult to mark out and quilt. The design in the sash rectangles does not easily fit within the graph paper lines. I knew that drawing the design would be more time intensive because I would need to measure instead of using point-to-point lines from the piecing.

The second drawing of BIG BERTHA'S quilting (fig. 12, p. 19) was the winner for me because the design was going to be easier to mark. I changed the block size to 12" finished, which made the 4" sashing divisible to the block. Being able to divide my designs evenly and have them divisible makes my life easier. With this design, I was able to mark middle lines as a reference

Fig. 12

and use a point-to-point method to mark out the design. You will notice this in the project instructions when you are making your own quilt.

The first secondary design element in Big Bertha is shown in figure 13. The horizontal and vertical lines of the piecing are in the background and the on-point square design created on a 45° angle shines through as the secondary design. One of the things that I do when I have completed a quilt is to look at the secondary design that I have created and come up with more design ideas from the lines created. I log those ideas away in my memory, or draw them out, and use those ideas on another project. I am always building my design base, and a lot of my quilting designs come from inspiration on previous projects.

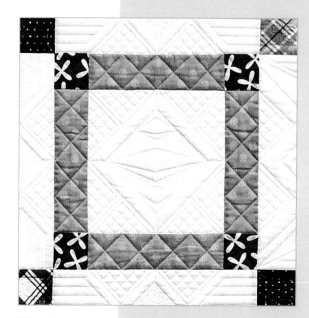

Fig. 13

Fig. 14

The next secondary design element in BIG BERTHA is the geometric flower that is created next to the sash squares (fig. 14). You can see how the center sash square is the center of the flower and the quilted straight lines on each side of the sash make the petal shape. I love being able to create several secondary design elements within each quilt top that I quilt. If I were to decide to change this area of the quilt and make it a little more "soft," I could quilt a feather motif in each of these petals. That would change the design enough to give you a whole new look on this incredible quilt design.

The final secondary design and the best part of the quilt, in my opinion, are the outside border sash rectangles. Instead of quilting the sash rectangles as I have quilted in the middle, I treated the outside sash rectangles like a pieced border. The quilting design gave the quilt a border that doubled as a secondary design (fig. 15).

I have shown you the three secondary designs in BIG BERTHA that I can see in the quilt top, but if you take a moment and look at the quilt and the lines from the secondary quilting, you could come up with several more ways to make this quilt top unique and different. Use your imagination, have fun with it, and create your own style of quilting. That is what I hope this book inspires you to do. Try new things and make it your own.

Fig. 15

THIS WAY

The project THIS WAY is an example of making a secondary quilting design out of nothing or no help from the piecing. I drew out this quilt several times and had a lot of ideas for the quilting and piecing (fig. 16). I talk about how the arrow was the inspiration for the design in the quilting instructions for this project. However, the first time I put this quilt idea together, it was going to be pieced much like my BIG BERTHA design, without the triangle piecing in the blocks. You can see in the original drawing (fig. 17) that I planned on quilting the triangles in the blocks for each empty square and from these triangles I was able to draw out the arrow into

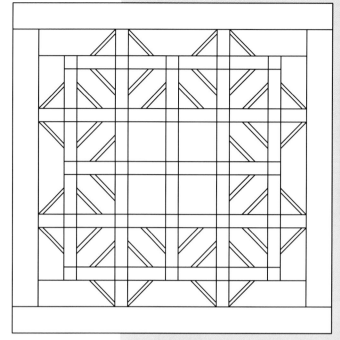

Fig. 16

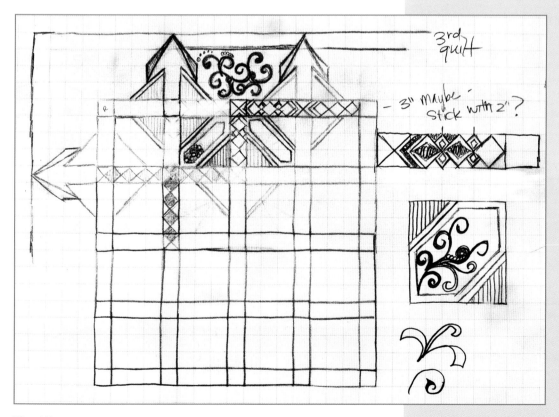

Fig. 17

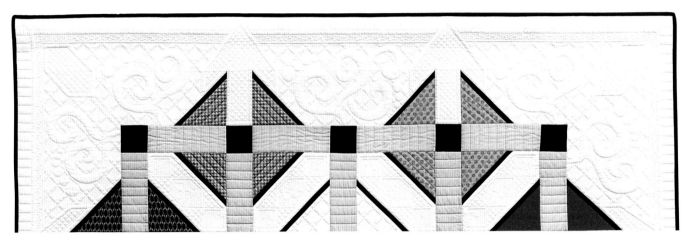

Fig. 18

Fig. 19

the borders. I was trying to piece the arrows in another mockup design before I even sketched this out, but then I realized how difficult it would be to figure it out, let alone explain it. So, by the process of elimination you end up with the design that was finalized in this book. I think I figured out the best possible scenario for this quilt. I hope you enjoy it.

The large Swirl designs were simplified for the pattern, but you can see the general idea was followed through in the design. The sash rectangles design was not even close to the original drawing. I chose a much simpler and more streamlined quilting design. Sometimes straight lines are all you need to balance the heavy detail of the quilting in the blocks.

The secondary design can be found in the borders of this quilt; the basket shapes as well as the arrows make for a fantastic secondary design (fig. 18). The piecing for this particular quilt is beautiful, but the secondary design in this quilt really makes it. I like to pull elements from the quilting or piecing to tie all the quilting together. You can see in the border corner designs that I have pulled the hexagon shape from the piecing blocks by quilting a hexagon in each corner. It serves as a break for the basket swirl shapes while complementing the pieced shapes in the quilt. It also has the same cross-hatch stitching that is in the arrows.

The center of the quilt pulls the whole quilting design together. By shrinking the swirl motif and crosshatch stitches, it pulls the border elements together. So keep that in mind when you design your quilts. Use the same elements, but just change the sizes. Also, in the background of this design, I have quilted the same large crosshatch that you find in the border. This ties the design in perfectly (fig. 19).

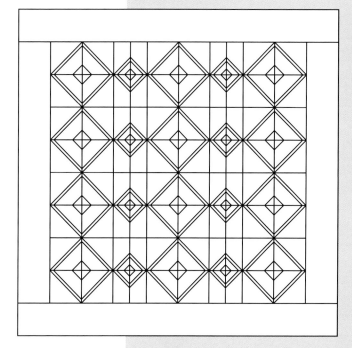

Fig. 20

NORTH STAR

This quilt is an example of using the pieced block as a way of connecting the secondary design (fig. 20). You can see how the quilting lines in the quilt pull each design element together to make an incredible background design for the entire center area of the quilt. The quilting lines connect from one block to the next, and it looks amazing just drawn out (fig. 21). Once you see the connecting lines quilted, you might just cry with how amazing it looks! See figure 22 on p. 24.

So, the next time you plan out the quilting on a quilt top, look beyond the blocks as individual quilting spaces and instead find a way

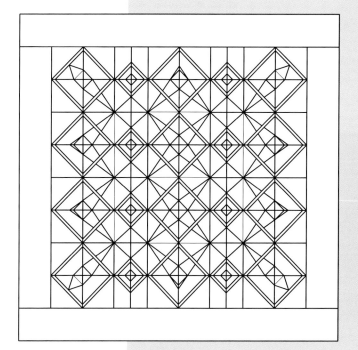

Fig. 21

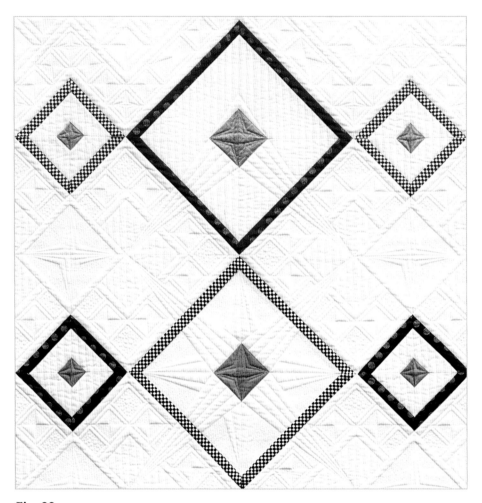

Fig. 22

to incorporate the entire quilt top by connecting the blocks in the background. You will be amazed at the difference it will make and will make quilting more enjoyable. I find that when I have some new design to try, I get more excited about the quilting, and I do not complain as much about how long it takes me to quilt it.

The balance of the quilting is apparent in NORTH STAR since the straight lines within the on-point squares separate the intense quilting next to it (fig. 22). I try to bring balance to all of my quilts by letting some areas breathe while quilting a lot of detail right next to it.

The quilting balance came easier for me as I quilted more, so do not worry if you struggle with that right now. Time and practice will help you become good at knowing what to quilt and where.

The last part of the secondary design in NORTH STAR that I want to discuss is the small border design. I chose to ignore the border seam allowances and followed the piecing instead. The lines created by following the on-point squares create an amazing border around the piecing which shows it off. You can see in figure 23 how the secondary border design enhances

Fig. 23

the pieced design, and because it borders the entire pieced design, it brings your attention to the piecing. You want to showcase the piecing by enhancing it with your quilting.

I must admit, I think this is my favorite quilt I have ever worked on. The design and quilting came out perfectly, and I hope you enjoy making this project.

PLAYTIME

Looking at this quilt top, you wouldn't know where the piecing was; that is the trick to secondary design for me. I don't allow the piecing to limit my areas of quilting design. I look at the background and see what shapes can be found and what lines can be connected. In PLAYTIME, I played with the piecing design and came up with the on-point square design to connect each block together as well as the borders (fig. 24).

See how the lines change the entire look of the quilt?

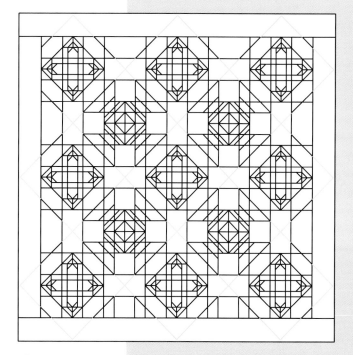

Fig. 24

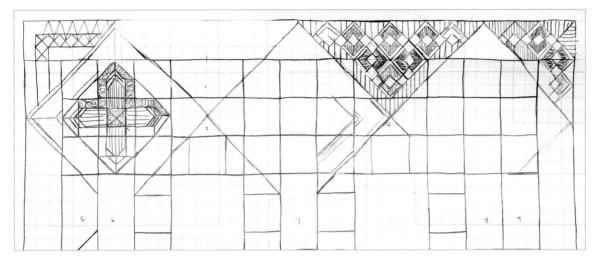

Fig. 25

Fig. 26

Now that I have the shape I want for the quilt, what am I going to quilt in the border? Well, that's when I pull out my graph paper again and start drawing out possible designs. It only took two tries for me to figure out which design to go with in the borders. The design on the left is fun, but would be super time consuming. The design on the right worked perfectly (fig. 25).

So, I have the outline shape of the secondary design. I have the border design. Now I am going to start quilting. I don't plan the entire quilting design for the quilt top because I want the quilt to speak to me. As I finished the top border of the quilt, I realized that the fun on-point little squares in the design were the perfect design to carry into the Cross blocks (fig. 26).

You can see in figure 26 that the squares in the Cross blocks mimic the shape of the squares in the border, so it definitely brings this design together. So, why stop there? I can use this same shape and design concept when I work on the Diamond blocks. You can see in figure 27 that I pulled the squares into the Diamond block, but I had to make them smaller because the area was smaller. This is another example of using the designs you have, but making them fit the area you are working on, bringing the design together.

The last thing that ties the design all together are the straight ½" lines. You can see I used the ½" spaced lines to offset the dense quilting in the Cross blocks, but I also used these lines because they were used in the border as well. I could have put other quilting in this area, but, because I put the lines in the edge of the quilt, I wanted to put it in the center as well to bring it all together (fig. 28).

I hope by explaining my thought process on each one of these designs it will help you to understand how I come up with designs for my quilts. I also hope that it inspires you to come up with your designs and gives you the encouragement you need to become a better quilter. We all have room for improvement and the best part about that is that it is fun. Quilting is so rewarding, and I am so grateful to be able to do something that I love.

Go! Have fun and enjoy the projects in this book. Give secondary designs a try and you will become hooked! I promise it's a good thing.

Fig. 27

Fig. 28

Projects

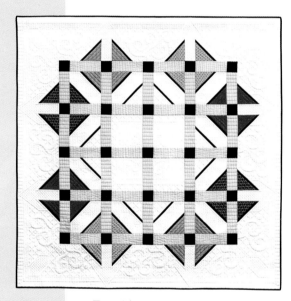

This Way, Project on the CD

Star X-ing, Project on the CD

Diamond in the Rough, 32" x 56"
Designed, pieced, and quilted by Judi Madsen

Diamond in the Rough

Fabric Requirements

Grey – 1⅞ yards

Dark Blue (includes binding) – 1 yard

Turquoise – 1¼ yards

Green – ⅓ yard

Blue Polka Dot – ⅛ yard

Backing – 1⅞ yards

Cutting and Preparation

GREY

Fifty-six (56) 4½" x 4½" squares for background fabric. Draw a diagonal line from corner to corner on the wrong side of the fabric on each square for the sewing line.

Sixteen (16) 7½" x 7½" squares for HSTs in Diamond blocks. Draw a diagonal line from corner to corner on the wrong side of the fabric on each square for the sewing line.

DARK BLUE

Eight (8) 7½" x 7½" squares for HSTs in Diamond blocks

Five (5) 2½" x width of fabric strips for binding

TURQUOISE

Eight (8) 7½" x 7½" squares for HSTs in Diamond blocks

Twenty-four (24) 4½" x 6½" rectangles for outside blocks

Four (4) 4½" x 4½" squares for corners

GREEN

Sixty-four (64) 2½" x 2½" squares for corner triangles in blocks. Draw a diagonal line from corner to corner on the wrong side of the fabric on each square for the sewing line.

BLUE POLKA DOT

Forty-eight (48) 1½" x 1½" squares for corner triangles in blocks. Draw a diagonal line from corner to corner on the wrong side of the fabric on each square for the sewing line.

 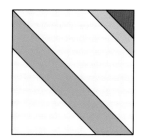

A Blocks. Make 8 of each.

A Block: You will need the following to make a total of sixteen (16) A blocks, eight (8) Dark Blue and eight (8) Turquoise

    Four (4) Turquoise 7½" squares

    Four (4) Dark blue 7½" squares

    Eight (8) Grey 7½" squares

    Sixteen (16) Grey 4½" squares

    Sixteen (16) Green 2½" squares

    Sixteen (16) Blue Polka Dot 1½" squares

Place a grey 7½" Grey square RST with a Dark Blue 7½" square. Sew ¼" away on both sides of the drawn line (fig. 1). Cut along line to get two HSTs. Press seams to one side (fig. 2).

Trim HSTs to 6½" x 6½" square.

Place a 4½" Grey square in the lower left corner on the Blue side of the HST (fig. 3).

Sew along the drawn line. Trim away excess fabric leaving a ¼" seam allowance. Press seam (fig. 4).

Place a Green 2½" square RST in the top right corner on the Grey fabric and sew along the drawn line (fig. 5). Trim excess fabric leaving a ¼" seam allowance. Press seam (fig. 6).

Place a 1½" Blue Polka Dot square RST in the top right corner on the Green fabric and sew along the drawn line (fig. 7). Trim excess fabric and press seam (fig. 8).

The finished block should be squared to 6½" x 6½".

You will make a total of eight (8) Dark Blue A blocks and eight (8) Turquoise A blocks. When pressing seam allowances press all seams to the left of four (4) Dark Blue blocks and four (4) Turquoise blocks. Press all seams of the remaining four (4) Dark

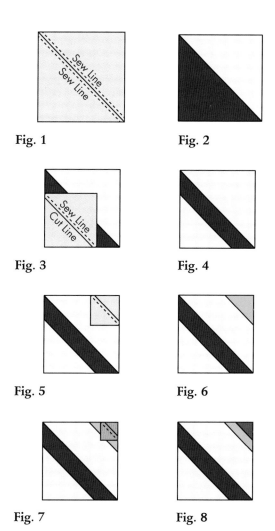

Fig. 1   Fig. 2

Fig. 3   Fig. 4

Fig. 5   Fig. 6

Fig. 7   Fig. 8

Blue and four (4) Turquoise A blocks to the right. This will make sure that your seam allowances will meet up just right.

B Block

B Block: You will need the following to make two (2) B blocks:
One (1) Grey 7½" square
One (1) Turquoise 7½" square
Two (2) Grey 4½" squares
Two (2) Blue Polka Dot 1½" squares
Four (4) Green 2½" squares

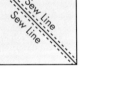

Fig. 9

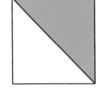

Fig. 10

Place a Grey 7½" Grey square RST with a Turquoise 7½" square. Sew ¼" away on both sides of the drawn line (fig. 9). Cut along the line to get two HSTs. Press seams to one side (fig. 10).

Trim HSTs to 6½" x 6½" square.

Fig. 11

Fig. 12

Place a 4½" Grey square in the upper right corner on the Turquoise side of the HST. Sew along the drawn line (fig. 11). Trim away excess fabric leaving a ¼" seam allowance. Press the seam (fig. 12).

Fig. 13

Fig. 14

Place a Green 2½" square on both sides of the block as shown to the left and sew along the drawn line on each square (fig. 13). Trim excess fabric leaving a ¼" seam allowance. Press seams (fig. 14).

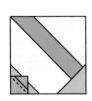

Fig. 15

Fig. 16

Place a Blue Polka Dot 1½" square on the left side of the Green fabric as shown. Sew along the drawn line (fig. 15). Trim excess fabric leaving a ¼" seam allowance and press the seams (fig. 16).

Press all seams in block B to the right.

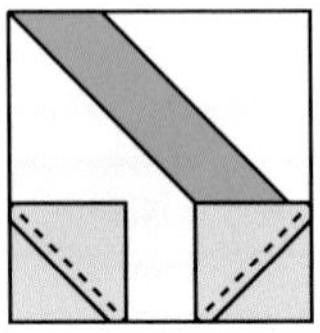

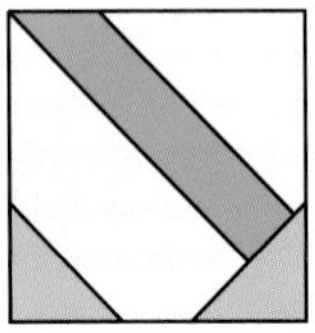

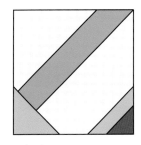

C Block

C Block: You will need the following to make two (2) C blocks:

One (1) Grey 7½" square

One (1) Turquoise 7½" square

Two (2) Grey 4½" squares

Two (2) Blue Polka Dot 1½" squares

Four (4) Green 2½" squares

Place a Grey 7½" Grey square RST with a Turquoise 7½" square. Sew ¼" away on both sides of the drawn line (fig. 17). Cut along the line to get two HSTs. Press seams to one side (fig. 18).

Trim HSTs to 6½" x 6½" square.

Place a 4½" Grey square in the upper left corner on the Turquoise side of the HST. Sew along the drawn line (fig. 19). Trim away excess fabric leaving a ¼" seam allowance. Press seam (fig. 20).

Place a Green 2½" square on both sides of the block and sew along the drawn line on each square (fig. 21). Trim excess fabric leaving a ¼" seam allowance. Press seams (fig. 22).

Place a Blue Polka Dot 1½" square on the right side of the Green fabric. Sew along the drawn line, (fig. 23). Trim excess fabric leaving a ¼" seam allowance and press seams (fig. 24).

Press all seams in C block to the left.

Fig. 17

Fig. 18

Fig. 19

Fig. 20

Fig. 21

Fig. 22

Fig. 23

Fig. 24

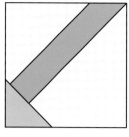

D Block

D Block: You will need the following to make four (4) Dark Blue D blocks and two (2) Turquoise D blocks:

Three (3) Grey 7½" squares

Six (6) Grey 4½" squares

Two (2) Dark Blue 7½" squares

One (1) Turquoise 7½" square

Six (6) Green 2½" squares

Fig. 25

Fig. 26

Place a 7½" Grey square RST with a Turquoise 7½" square. Sew ¼" away on both sides of the drawn line (fig. 25). Cut along the line to get two HSTs. Press seams to one side (fig. 26).

Fig. 27

Fig. 28

Trim HSTs to 6½" x 6½" square.

Place a 4½" Grey square in the upper left corner on the Turquoise side of the HST. Sew along the drawn line (fig. 27). Trim away excess fabric leaving a ¼" seam allowance. Press seam (fig. 28).

Fig. 29

Fig. 30

Place a Green 2½" square on the lower left corner of the block and sew along the drawn line (fig. 29). Trim excess fabric leaving a ¼" seam allowance. Press seam (fig. 30).

Press all seams in D block to the left. You will make (four 4) Dark Blue D blocks and two (2) Turquoise D blocks.

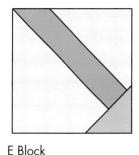

E Block

E Block: You will need the following to make four (4) Dark Blue E blocks and two (2) Turquoise E blocks:

Three (3) Grey 7½" squares

Six (6) Grey 4½" squares

Two (2) Dark Blue 7½" squares

One (1) Turquoise 7½" square

Six (6) Green 2½" squares

Place a 7½" Grey square RST with a Turquoise 7½" square. Sew ¼" away on both sides of the drawn line (fig. 31). Cut along the line to get two HSTs. Press seams to one side (fig. 32).

Trim HSTs to 6½" x 6½" square.

Place a 4½" Grey square in the upper right corner on the Turquoise side of the HST. Sew along the drawn line (fig. 33). Trim away excess fabric leaving a ¼" seam allowance. Press the seam (fig. 34).

Place a Green 2½" square on the lower right corner of the block. Sew along drawn line (fig. 35). Trim excess fabric leaving a ¼" seam allowance. Press the seam (fig. 36).

Press all seams in E block to the right. You will make four (4) Dark Blue E blocks and two (2) Turquoise E blocks.

Fig. 31

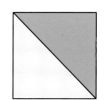

Fig. 32

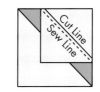

Fig. 33

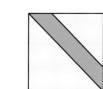

Fig. 34

Fig. 35

Fig. 36

F Block

F Block: Make four (4) blocks. You will need the following to make these blocks:

Four (4) Turquoise 4½" squares

Four (4) Green 2½" squares

Four (4) Blue Polka Dot 1½" squares

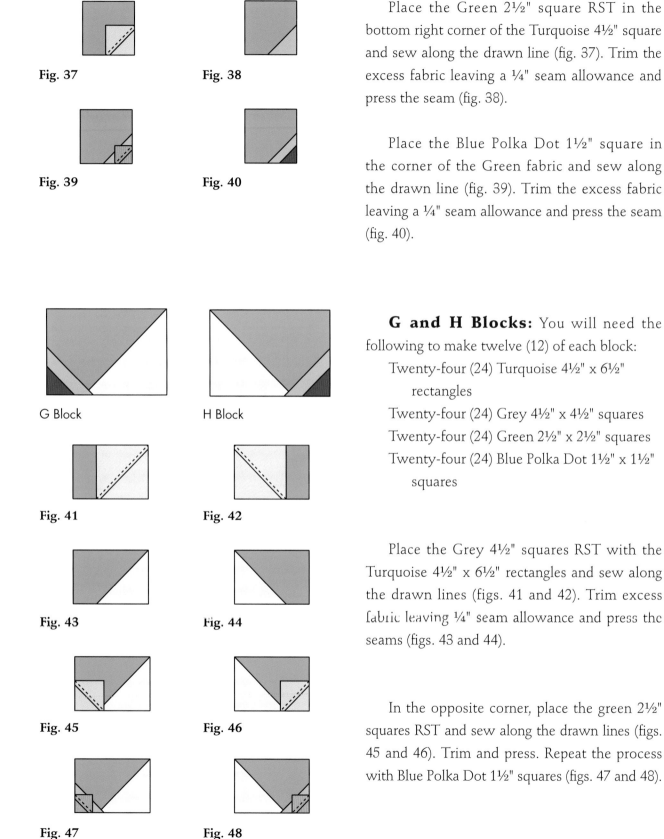

Fig. 37

Fig. 38

Fig. 39

Fig. 40

G Block

H Block

Fig. 41

Fig. 42

Fig. 43

Fig. 44

Fig. 45

Fig. 46

Fig. 47

Fig. 48

Place the Green 2½" square RST in the bottom right corner of the Turquoise 4½" square and sew along the drawn line (fig. 37). Trim the excess fabric leaving a ¼" seam allowance and press the seam (fig. 38).

Place the Blue Polka Dot 1½" square in the corner of the Green fabric and sew along the drawn line (fig. 39). Trim the excess fabric leaving a ¼" seam allowance and press the seam (fig. 40).

G and H Blocks: You will need the following to make twelve (12) of each block:
    Twenty-four (24) Turquoise 4½" x 6½" rectangles
    Twenty-four (24) Grey 4½" x 4½" squares
    Twenty-four (24) Green 2½" x 2½" squares
    Twenty-four (24) Blue Polka Dot 1½" x 1½" squares

Place the Grey 4½" squares RST with the Turquoise 4½" x 6½" rectangles and sew along the drawn lines (figs. 41 and 42). Trim excess fabric leaving ¼" seam allowance and press the seams (figs. 43 and 44).

In the opposite corner, place the green 2½" squares RST and sew along the drawn lines (figs. 45 and 46). Trim and press. Repeat the process with Blue Polka Dot 1½" squares (figs. 47 and 48).

Press seams in eight (8) of the G blocks to the right and the seams in four (4) of the G blocks to the left (fig. 49).

Press seams in eight (8) of the H blocks to the left and the seams in four (4) of the H blocks to the right (fig. 50).

The blocks should all be put together now. Time to lay out the quilt. As long as the seams have been pressed to the sides that have been explained throughout this pattern, the seams should nestle into each other nicely. When laying the quilt out, pay attention to the seam allowance and be sure to pin seams well. Assemble the quilt top in rows. Use layout (fig. 51) for placement.

Now to quilt!

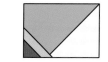

Fig. 49

Fig. 50

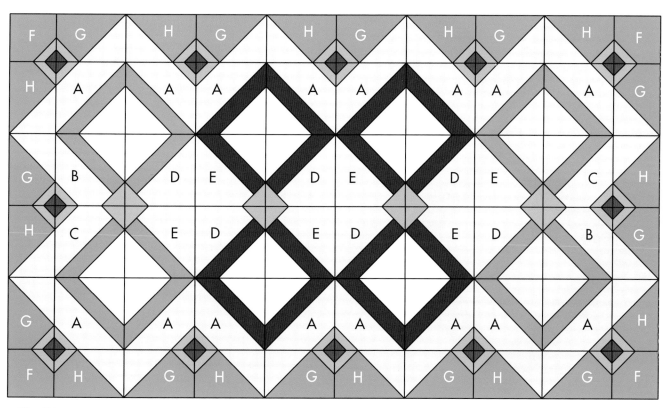

Fig. 51

Quilting Diamond in the Rough

This particular quilt is so fun to quilt up. Since it is a smaller project, you should not experience burnout with this design. At least for me, I had fun for the entire quilting process. It has a lot of fine stitching and some areas of thread build-up. For that reason I used Kimono Silk thread by Superior Threads. It is one of my favorite fine 100-weight threads to use. I use the thread in the top as well as in the bobbin. You will most likely need to wind your bobbins, but be sure to wind the thread slowly because the thread is so fine. It can push out your bobbin sides making the bobbin too large. Your bobbin will then not fit in your bobbin case. I learned that from experience!

Now would be an excellent time for you to try quilting with two layers of batting. I used two layers of Hobbs wool for this project. However, if you have not quilted with two layers of batting before, you should not try wool first. I recommend using a layer of 80/20 cotton-poly blend as well as 100% cotton for your two layers. Keep the stronger 80/20 cotton-poly blend batting as the bottom layer and the 100% cotton batting as the top layer. Okay, let's begin!

There will be three fillers within this project: The **Side-to-Side** (fig. 52, p. 39); the **Pebble** (fig. 53, p. 39); and the **Scribble-Pebble** (fig. 54, p. 39). These types of fillers take a little more time, but they are perfect for this project and will be well worth your effort. The examples within the quilt are shown on p. 39.

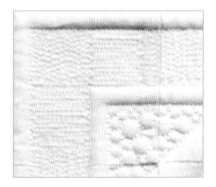

Fig. 52. The Side-to-Side

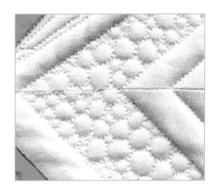

Fig. 53. The Pebble

Fig. 54. The Scribble-Pebble

Drawing and Quilting

Let's get started!

Use the diagram for placement (fig. 55). Each section drawn is color coordinated and corresponds with a numbering system. I will give you the drawing instructions with the quilting path instructions for some of the harder sections, but the easier sections should be able to be quilted without a step by step. Just remember that stitch in the ditch is your friend and that traveling over previous stitches isn't a problem, especially with 100-weight thread.

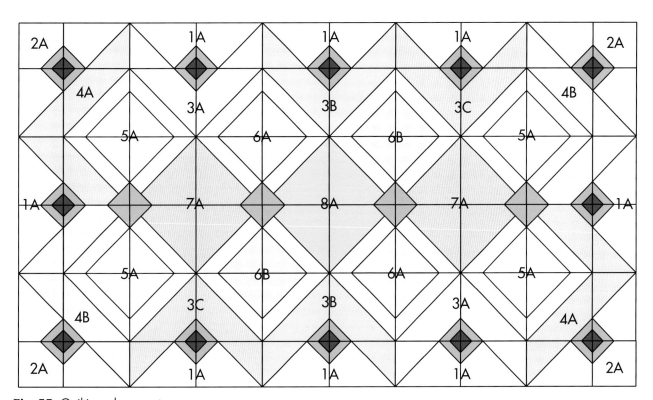

Fig. 55. Quilting placement

DRAWING FOR THE OUTSIDE BORDER (fig. 56, 1A)

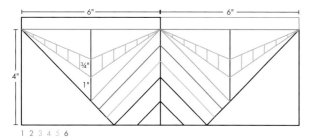

Fig. 56. Outside Border drawing 1A. Drawing is full size on the CD.

1. Using the seams allowance on the G and H Blocks as a guideline, measure 4" and draw a line at the top of the quilt blocks as shown in Green. This line will be your guideline to keep the stitches in the ditch.

2. Draw a vertical line in the center of each G and H block as shown in Purple.

3. Draw two diagonal lines to make an upside down V mimicking the Green on-point square in the block. The lines will start where the center Purple lines are drawn and up to the center seam allowance of the blocks as shown in Orange.

4. Draw two upside down V's to mimic the lines drawn in step 3, ⅜" away from the Orange lines and ⅜" away from the Green fabric on-point square as shown in Aqua.

5. On the Blue center line measure out 1" from the triangle point and put a mark, then from the 1" mark measure out ¾" and draw a mark. Now draw a line from these marks to the outside seam allowances as well as the center

seam allowance as shown in Pink. Do this for both sides of the on-point square.

6. Starting from the center out, draw a ½" line in between the two Pink lines drawn in step 5 as shown in Purple.

QUILTING PATHS FOR OUTSIDE BORDER

All the quilting path instructions are continuous. Make sure you have your needle in the down position when you stop for the best results (1B, fig. 57; 1C, fig. 58; and 1D, fig. 59).

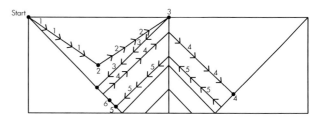

Fig. 57. Outside Border diagram 1B. Diagram is full size on the CD.

1. Start at the top left corner point #1 and stitch one diagonal straight line to point #2.

2. Stitch one diagonal straight line to point #3.

3. Continue stitching diagonal straight lines, following the arrows in the diagram to point #4.

4. Stitch diagonal straight lines to point #5.

5. Take a small stitch up to point #6.

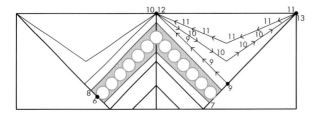

Fig. 58. Outside Border diagram 1C. Diagram is full size on the CD.

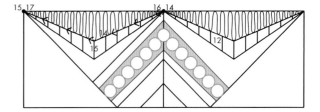

Fig. 59. Outside Border diagram 1D. Diagram is full size on the CD.

6. Free motion stitch circles within the lines as shown to point #7 (fig. 58).

7. Free motion stitch a **Scribble** filler between one side of the circles and the inside line to point #8.

8. Free motion stitch a **Scribble** filler between the other side of the circles and the outside line to point #9.

9. Stitch a diagonal straight line up and to the left to point #10.

10. Stitch two (2) diagonal straight lines left to right to point #11.

11. Stitch two (2) diagonal straight lines right to left to point #12.

12. Traveling over previous stitch lines, stitch the ½" straight lines in between the two lines that make the V shape to point #13.

13. Free motion quilt an up-and-down stitch as shown in the diagram to point #14 or center seam allowance (fig. 59).

14. Stitch two diagonal straight lines from right to left to point #15.

15. Traveling over previous stitch lines, stitch the ½" straight lines in between the two lines that make the V shape to point #16.

16. Free motion quilt an up-and-down stitch to point #17 to finish.

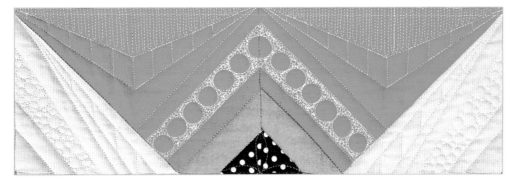

Fig. 60. Example of quilted outside border

DRAWING CORNER BORDER DESIGN

1. Draw 4" from the inside seam allowance to the edge of the quilt as shown in Green. This will give you your quilting reference or stop line (fig. 61).

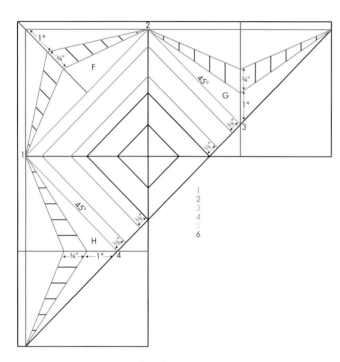

Fig. 61. Corner Border diagram 2A. Diagram is full size on the CD.

Fig. 62. Corner Border design drawn on quilt

2. Divide each H and G block in half at 3" and draw a straight line as shown in Blue. Draw a 45-degree straight line in the center of the F block as shown in Blue.

3. In the F block, draw a diagonal straight line from point #1 to point #2 as shown in Orange. Draw a straight diagonal 45-degree line from point #2 down to point #3 as shown in Orange in the G block. Draw a diagonal straight 45-degree line from point #1 to point #4 as shown in Orange in the H block.

4. Mimicking the Orange lines drawn in step 3, come in ⅜" and draw three lines as shown in Aqua. Repeat this step, but come out ⅜" from the seam allowance from the Green on-point fabric square as shown in Aqua.

5. In blocks G and H draw a reference point 1" from the point of the triangle and on the Blue center line, then draw another reference point ¾" from the 1" reference point. Connect these reference points with straight lines from the outside seam allowances to the center point as shown in Pink. In the F block draw a 1" reference point from the corner of the inside Green line drawn and on the center Blue line, then draw another reference point ¾" from the 1" reference point. Connect these reference points with straight lines from the outside seam allowances to the center point as shown in Pink.

6. In between the two triangle lines drawn in each block from step 5, draw ½" lines from the center point as shown in Purple.

QUILTING PATH FOR CORNER BORDER DESIGN

1. Start stitching at point #1 in the lower left corner of the H block. Stitch the middle straight diagonal line up and to the right and then stitch another straight diagonal line up and to the left to point #2 as shown in Pink (fig. 63).

2. Stitch a straight diagonal line down and to the right, then stitch another straight diagonal down and to the left to point #3 as shown in Pink.

3. Travel on the lines stitched in steps 1 and 2 and stitch the ½" lines in between the two lines to point #4 as shown in Yellow.

4. Free motion stitch a back and forth squiggle lines to point #5 as shown in Green.

5. Stitch a diagonal straight line in the ditch up and to the right as shown in Blue. Continue stitching the outside lines of the on-point square to point #6 as shown in Blue.

6. Stitch the inside lines of the on-point square to point #7 as shown in Purple.

7. Stitch the other lines of the on-point square to point #8 as shown in Pink.

8. Free motion stitch circles in between the two lines from the previous steps, stitching to point #9 as shown in Orange.

9. Free motion stitch **Scribbles** on the inside of the circles and in between the lines as shown in Yellow to point #10.

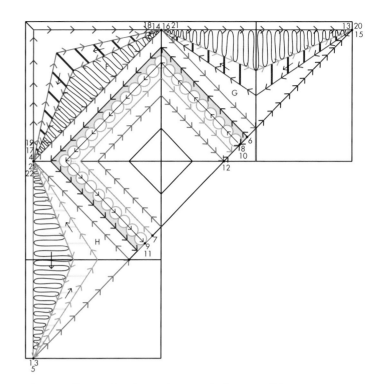

Fig. 63. Corner Border quilting path diagram 2B. Diagram is full size on the CD.

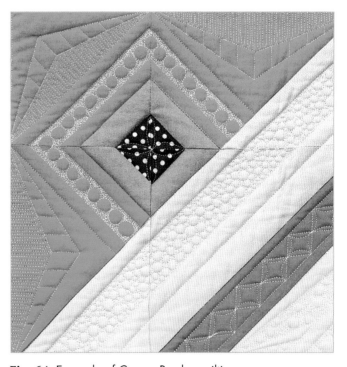

Fig. 64. Example of Corner Border quilting

10. Continue **Scribble** stitches on the other side of the circles and in between the lines and stitch to point #11 as shown in Green.

11. Stitch straight lines in the ditch around the Green fabric square to point #12 as shown in Blue.

12. Stitch a diagonal straight line in the ditch to point #13 as shown in Purple.

13. Stitch the middle diagonal straight line down and to the left, then stitch another straight diagonal line up and to the left to point #14 as shown in Red.

14. Stitch a diagonal straight line down and to the right, then stitch another straight diagonal line up and to the right to point #15 as shown in Orange.

15. Travel on the lines stitched in steps 13 and 14 and stitch the ½" lines in between the two lines to point #16 as shown in Purple.

16. Stitch the middle straight diagonal lines in block F down and to the left to point #17 as shown in Green.

17. Stitch diagonal lines up and to the right to point #18 as shown in Blue.

18. Travel on the lines stitched in steps 15 and 16 and stitch the ½" lines in between the two lines to point #19 as shown in Purple.

19. Stitch straight lines up, then to the right to point #20 as shown in Red.

20. Free motion stitch up-and-down squiggle lines from right to left to point #21 as shown in Orange.

21. Free motion stitch a diagonal squiggle line to point #22 as shown in Yellow for the finish!

DRAWING AND QUILTING FOR SECTION 3A

Pay attention to the diagram for the correct measurements and points (fig. 65).

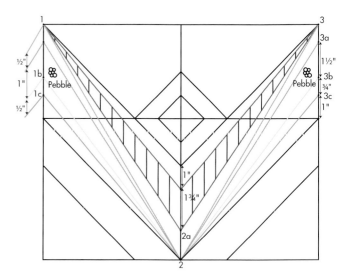

Fig. 65. Section 3A quilting diagram. Diagram is full size on the CD.

1. Draw a diagonal line from point #1 to point #2, then continue with another diagonal line from point #2 to point #3 as shown in Red.

2. To start this line you will need to reference diagram 4A (p. 47 and CD) for the Grey area lines. Start at point #1a which is the ½" line from 4A and draw a straight diagonal line down to point #2. Continue with another diagonal line from point #2 to point #3a as shown in Orange.

3. Draw a diagonal straight line from point #1b to point #2, then continue with a straight diagonal line to point #3b as shown in Yellow.

4. Draw a diagonal straight line from point #1c to point #2, then continue with a straight diagonal line to point #3c as shown in Green.

5. Draw a diagonal straight line from point #1 to point #2a, then continue with a straight diagonal line to point #3. Draw another diagonal straight line from point #1 to point #2b, then continue with a straight diagonal line to point #3 as shown in Blue.

6. Draw vertical lines ½" apart starting in the center as shown in Purple, in between the Blue lines drawn in step #5.

7. Quilt the straight lines, **Pebble** in between the Orange and Yellow lines.

DRAWING AND QUILTING FOR SECTION 3B

Use the points in the blocks for the best drawing results and pay attention to the diagram (fig. 66). Some of these lines will also be included in other diagrams, but will help with the drawing in this section. Dotted lines are for drawing line reference and are not quilted lines.

1. Use the 6" A block points to draw a straight diagonal line from point #1 to point #2, then continue a straight diagonal line from point #2 to point #3 as shown in Red.

2. Draw a straight diagonal line ½" away from the first line from point #4 to point #5, then continue the straight line from point #5 to point #6 as shown in Orange.

3. Draw a straight diagonal line 1" away from the previous line from point #7 to point #8,

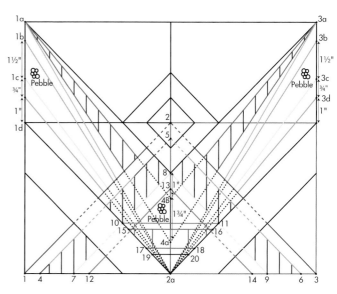

Fig. 66. Section 3B quilting diagram. Diagram is full size on the CD.

then continue the straight line from point #8 to point #9 as shown in Yellow.

4. Draw a horizontal straight line from point #10 to point #11 as shown in Green.

5. Draw a straight diagonal line ½" away from the Yellow line from step 3, from point #12 to point #13, then continue the straight line to point #14 as shown in Green.

6. Draw a horizontal straight line ¼" away from the Green line drawn in step 4 from point #15 to point #16 as shown in Blue. Draw another horizontal straight line ¾" away from previous line from point #17 to point #18 as shown in Blue. Then draw vertical straight lines in between the two lines ¾" apart as shown in Blue. You will quilt an up-and-down, side-to-side stitch filler in this section.

7. Draw a horizontal straight line ¼" away from the Blue line from point #19 to point #20 as shown in Purple.

8. Draw a diagonal straight line from point #1a to point #2a, then continue the straight line from #2a to point #3a as shown in Red. Keep in mind the dotted lines are for reference, and don't need to be drawn. Stop your line at the Red diagonal line from step 1. This will apply to the rest of the drawing instructions for this section.

9. Draw a diagonal straight line from point #1b to point #2a, then continue the straight line from 2a, to point #3b as shown in Orange.

10. Draw a diagonal straight line from point #1c to point #2a, then continue the straight line from point #2a to point #3c as shown in Yellow.

11. Draw a diagonal straight line from point #1d to point #2a, then continue the straight line from point #2a to point #3d as shown in Green.

12. Draw a diagonal straight line from point #1a to point #4a, then continue the straight line from point #4a to point #3a as shown in Blue. Draw another diagonal straight line from point #1a to point #4b, then continue the straight line from #4b to point #3a as shown in Blue.

13. Draw vertical straight lines ½" apart starting from the center seam in the block. Draw the lines in between the two diagonal lines just drawn as well as in between the 1" Orange and Yellow diagonal lines drawn in steps 2 and 3. The lines are shown in Purple.

14. Quilt the straight lines, **Pebble** in between the Orange and Yellow lines. **Pebble** in the Green triangle space and stitch an up-and-down filler in the Blue ¾" squares from step 6.

DRAWING FOR SECTION 3C

This section is a mirror image of section 3A and can be drawn following the 3C diagram and instructions from 3A. Full-size diagram 3C is on the CD.

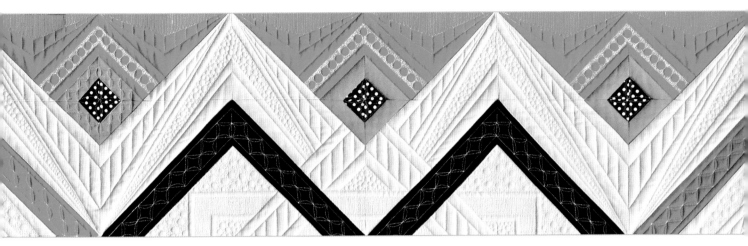

Fig. 67. Example of Sections 3A, 3B, and 3C quilting

DRAWING AND QUILTING FOR SECTION 4A

Drawing shouldn't be a problem with this section, but it can get a little tricky with the quilting. When you are quilting long straight lines, it is important to have a steady hand. I like to quilt my straight lines in good runs about 8" long. My ruler is 9" long and is the right size for control. If you need to break up the quilting lines, pause at seams, then continue. Hopefully that will help eliminate wobbly lines.

1. Draw a diagonal line from point #1a to point #2a, then continue with a straight diagonal line from point #2a to point #3 as shown in Orange (fig. 68).

2. Draw a diagonal line 1" away from the Orange line starting from point #1b to point #2b, then continue with a straight diagonal line from point #2b to point #3 as shown in Yellow.

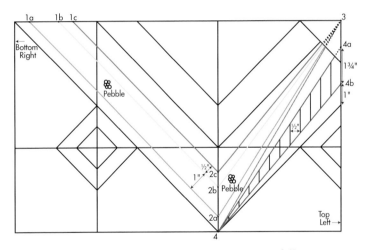

Fig. 68. Section 4A quilting diagram. Diagram is full size on the CD.

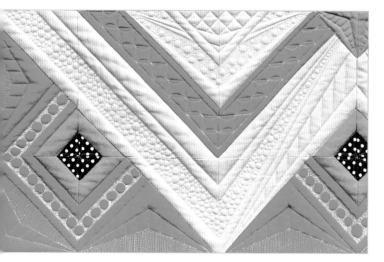

Fig. 69. Example of Sections 4A quilting

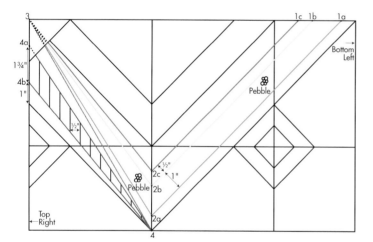

Fig. 70. Section 4B quilting diagram. Diagram is full size on the CD.

3. Draw a diagonal line ½" away from the Yellow line starting from point #1c to point #2c, then continue with a straight line from point #2c to point #3 as shown in Green.

4. Draw a diagonal straight line from point #3 to point #4 as shown in Red.

5. Draw a diagonal straight line from point #4 to point #4a as shown in Blue. Draw another straight diagonal line from point #4 to point #4b as shown in Blue.

6. Draw vertical lines ½" apart as shown in Purple in between the Blue lines drawn in step 5.

7. Quilt the straight lines, then **Pebble** between the Orange and Yellow lines.

DRAWING AND QUILTING FOR SECTION 4B

This section is a mirror image of section 4A and can be drawn following the 4B diagram and instructions from 4A (fig. 47).

DRAWING INSTRUCTIONS FOR SECTION 5A

These instructions will include the drawing and quilting path for the inside design of the on-point diamonds. You will quilt this particular design in each of the 8 point-on-point diamonds. It will also include the quilting and quilting path for the inside design of the on-point diamond. Pay attention to the measurements and points in the diagrams (fig. 71 and fig. 72).

1. Draw a line ¼" on each side and in from the seam of the on-point diamond shape as shown in Red. These two lines should be 1" apart.

2. Draw lines in between the Red lines at roughly 1". You may need to have a couple of the squares just bigger than 1" to work. Use the diagram (5A) to know how many lines to have in each section of the on-point square.

3. Starting at point #1, draw a diagonal line up to point #2, then continue with another straight line up to point #3 as shown in Yellow. Make two mirror lines like this in the block.

4. Coming in 1¾" from each point in the square, draw a smaller on-point square as shown in Green.

5. Draw another on-point square ½" smaller and on the inside of the Green square as shown in Blue.

6. Draw two mirroring lines from point #1 to point #4, then continue to point #3 as shown in Purple.

7. Draw two mirroring lines from point #1 to point #5, ⅜" from point #4, then continue to point #3 as shown in Red.

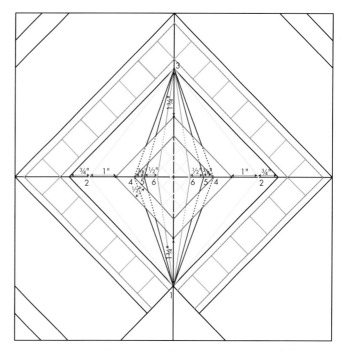

Fig. 71. Section 5A quilting diagram. Diagram is full size on the CD.

Fig. 72. Inside design drawing for the on-point diamonds

Fig. 73. Example of on-point triangle connecting curve design

8. Draw two mirroring lines from point #1 to point #6, ½" from point #5, then continue to point # 3 as shown in Orange.

9. Draw ½" crosshatch lines inside the shape made from the Orange lines and Blue square, shown in Yellow.

5B QUILTING PATH INSTRUCTIONS
Outside On-point Triangle Connecting Curve Design

1. Stitch straight diagonal lines from point #1, all the way to point #10 like a dot-to-dot following the arrows, then back to point #1 as shown in Red (fig. 74, p. 51).

2. Stitch stair-step straight stitches from point #1 in between the vertical lines between the Red lines. Work your way around the on-point square to point #6 as shown in Orange.

3. Continue stitching stair-step straight stitches between the lines to make a complete X in each 1" square and work your way back to point #10 as shown in Yellow.

4. Free motion stitch connecting curve lines between the triangle and on-point squares within the 1" squares. First stitch the Green lines as shown to point #11, then work your way back the other way to point #10 as shown in Blue. This will complete the connecting curve portion of the continuous path quilting design. You will do this same stitching in all eight sections like this.

Inside On-Point Square Quilting Design

1. Stitch a straight diagonal line up and to the left from point #1a to point #2a; continue stitching a straight diagonal line up and to the right from point #2a to point #3a. From point #3a stitch a straight diagonal line down and to the right to point #4a, then continue stitching a straight line down and to the left from point #4a back to point #1a as shown in Pink (fig. 74 and fig. 75).

2. Stitch a line up and to the left to point #5a, then continue the straight line stitch around the left side of the square up to point #6a as shown in Orange.

3. Straight stitch the three lines from point #6a to point #3a, then continue stitching down to point #7a as shown in Yellow.

4. Straight stitch the three lines from point #7a to point #3a, then continue stitching down to point #8a as shown in Green.

5. Stitch the three lines on the right of the square, then continue stitching around the last corner of the square up to point #5a. Then catch the remaining two straight diagonal lines, then back up to point #5a as seen in Blue.

6. Free motion quilt the **Scribble-Pebble** filler in all the negative space in the block as shown in Purple.

7. Stabilize your stitch, then drag your thread to point #9a and continue stitching the inside square straight lines as seen in Red and Orange.

Fig. 74. Section 5B quilting path diagram. Diagram is full size on the CD.

Fig. 75. Example of inside on-point triangle connecting curve design.

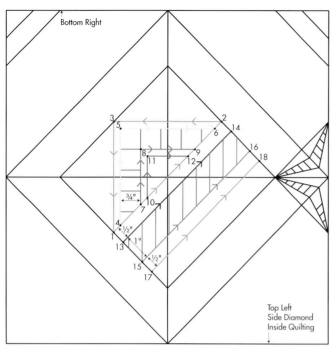

Fig. 76. Section 6A quilting path diagram. Diagram is full size on the CD.

Fig. 77. Example of quilting detail for 6A and 6B

DRAWING FOR SECTION 6A

1. Draw a straight diagonal line in the center of the on-point square from point #1 to point #2 as shown in Orange (fig. 76).

2. Draw a horizontal straight line from point #2 to point #3, then continue a straight vertical line down from point #3 back to point #1 as shown in Orange.

3. Draw a straight line ¼" to the right side of the Orange line from point #4 to point #5, then continue a straight line to point #6 as shown in Yellow.

4. Draw a straight line ¾" to the right side of the Yellow line from point #7 to point #8, then continue a straight line to point #9 as shown in Green. Draw straight lines in between the ¾" lines to make equal ¾" squares as shown in Green.

5. Draw a straight line ¼" to the right side of the Green line from point #10 to point #11, then continue a straight line to point #12 as shown in Blue.

6. Draw a straight diagonal line to the right and ½" to the side of the diagonal line drawn in step 1 from point #13 to point #14 as shown in Purple.

7. Draw a straight diagonal line to the right and 1" to the side of the diagonal line drawn in step 6 from point #15 to point #16 as shown in Pink. Draw vertical lines ½" apart in between the Purple and Pink lines drawn as shown in Pink.

8. Draw a straight diagonal line to the right and ½" to the side of the diagonal line drawn in step 7 from point #17 to point #18 as shown in Orange.

DRAWING FOR SECTION 6B

This section is a mirror image of section 6A and can be drawn following the 6B diagram (fig. 78) and instructions from 6A.

QUILTING 6A AND 6B

1. Stitch in the ditch around the Grey square, then start the first straight stitch at point #1 and stitch a diagonal line down to point #2.

2. Stitch a horizontal line from point #2 to point #3. Continue by stitching a vertical straight line from point #3 back up to point #1.

3. Free motion fill the empty space with a **Scribble-Pebble** design as shown in the diagram (fig. 78). Work your way to point #6. Stitch a straight line from point #6 to point #5, then continue a straight line to point #4.

4. Stitch to point #7, then stitch straight lines from point #7 to point #8 then on to point #9. Continue by quilting a free-motion "side-to-side, up-and-down" stitch in each of the ¾" squares as shown in the diagram (fig. 78). Work your way to point #4, then travel down to point #10.

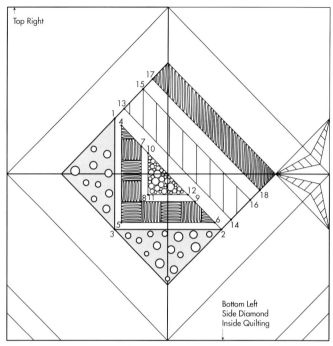

Fig. 78. Section 6B quilting diagram. Diagram is full size on the CD.

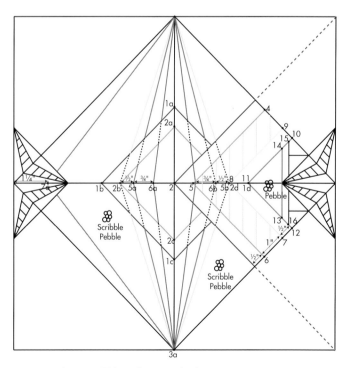

Fig. 79. Section 7A quilting path diagram. Diagram is full size on the CD.

5. Stitch a straight line from point #10 to point #11, then to point #12 as shown. Fill in the triangle space with free-motion **Pebbles** as shown.

6. Travel along the straight stitch to get back to point #1, then up to point #13. Stitch a straight diagonal line from point #13 to point #14. Travel up to point #16 then stitch a straight diagonal line from point #16 to point #15 and work back to point #13.

7. Stitch the vertical straight ½" lines in between the 1" section as shown and work your way to point #16.

8. Stitch up to point #18, then stitch a diagonal straight line from point #18 to point #17 and finish this block by stitching an up-and-down free-motion stitch in the remaining empty space as shown in the diagram (fig. 79, p. 53).

DRAWING FOR SECTION 7A

Please remember that the dotted lines in the diagrams are not quilting lines, but references for drawing. Pay attention to the measurements and point placements.

1. Start at point #1 and draw a diagonal line to the center of the block to point #2, then continue from point #2 to point #3 as shown in Red (fig. 79, p. 53 and figs. 80 and 81, p. 55).

2. Draw a line ½" to the right of the Red line just drawn starting at point #4 to point #5,

continuing to point #6 as shown in Orange.

3. Draw a straight line 1" to the right of the Orange line just drawn from point #7 to point #8, then to point #9 as shown in Yellow. Draw vertical lines ½" apart inside the 1" section as shown in Yellow.

4. Draw a straight line ½" to the right of the Yellow line from point #10 to point #11, then to point #12 as shown in Green.

5. Draw a straight vertical line from point #13 to point #14 as shown in Blue.

6. Draw a straight line ¼" to the right of the Blue line from point #15 to point #16 as shown in Purple. Draw two horizontal lines to the right of the Purple line as shown. This section will be filled in with free-motion up-and-down, side-to-side stitches.

7. Measure 2¾" from the center point (#2) horizontally and vertically in each direction and draw a mark. Connect these dots to make an on-point square with straight lines as shown in Red as points #1a, #1b, #1c and #1d.

8. Draw a smaller on-point square inside and ½" from the Red lines as shown as points #2a, #2b, #2c, and #2d in Orange.

9. Draw the outside diamond lines from point #3a to point #2b, then from #2b to point #4a. Continue from point #4a to point #2d, then from point #2d back to point #3a as shown in Yellow.

10. Draw the middle diamond lines from point #3a to point #5a to point #4a. Continue from point #4a to point #5b to point #3a as shown in Green.

11. Draw the inside diamond lines from point #3a to point #6a to point #4a. Continue from point #4a to point #6b to point #3a as shown in Blue. Draw ½" crosshatch lines in the square and in between the Blue diamond lines just drawn as shown in Blue.

12. Draw a straight diagonal line from point #3a to point #7a, then continue to point #4a as shown in Blue.

Fig. 80. Drawing of Section 7A

DRAWING FOR SECTION 7B

This section is a mirror image of section 7A and can be drawn following the 7A diagram and instructions from 7A.

The quilting in this section can be done almost in the same movement as the drawing instructions. It is also similar to the stitch path in section 5B, so you should be a pro by now. Stitch in the ditch around the Grey area, then work your way with the straight lines, then free motion fill the quilting designs when necessary. Use the picture of the quilting (fig. 81) as a reference and have fun!

DRAWING FOR CENTER SECTION 8A

1. From the edge of the seam allowance draw a line 1" away to mimic the shape of the Grey fabric shape as shown in Red (fig. 82, p. 56).

Fig. 81. Example of quilting Section 7A

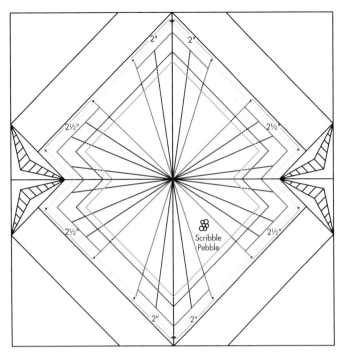

Fig. 82. Section 8A quilting path diagram of the center block. Diagram is full size on the CD.

Fig. 83. Example of quilting Section 8A quilt center

2. Draw another shape just inside the Red lines ¼" away as shown in Orange.

3. Draw the edge of the diamond (a) and fan (b) shapes within the design. For the "a" shapes draw a line ¼" away from the outside seams and 2½" to the ends of both sides of the shape, then draw two lines connecting to the center seam ¼" away from outside seam. For the "b" shapes draw a line ¼" away from the outside seams and 2" from the center seam to the end of the shape as shown in Yellow.

4. Connect the lines drawn in step 3 with diagonal straight lines drawn to the center of the Grey shape as shown in Green.

5. Draw a line on the inside of the Yellow lines and ¼" away as shown in Blue.

6. Divide the shapes with lines going from the Blue lines to the center seam. There will be two lines in the "b" shapes and six lines in the "a" shape as shown in Purple. Notice that you don't draw through the Red and Orange lines. The drawing is complete

7. For the quilting in this project I would start with the Red straight line shape, working my way around the edge of the design and catching the lines outside of the Red line of the "a" and "b" shapes. Once the outside straight line quilting is finished, then free motion quilt the **Scribble-Pebble** in the negative space. Now, pick up your needle and stitch the Orange straight line shape, work your way to each area and straight line within the shapes, then free motion quilt the **Scribble-Pebble** in the negative space.

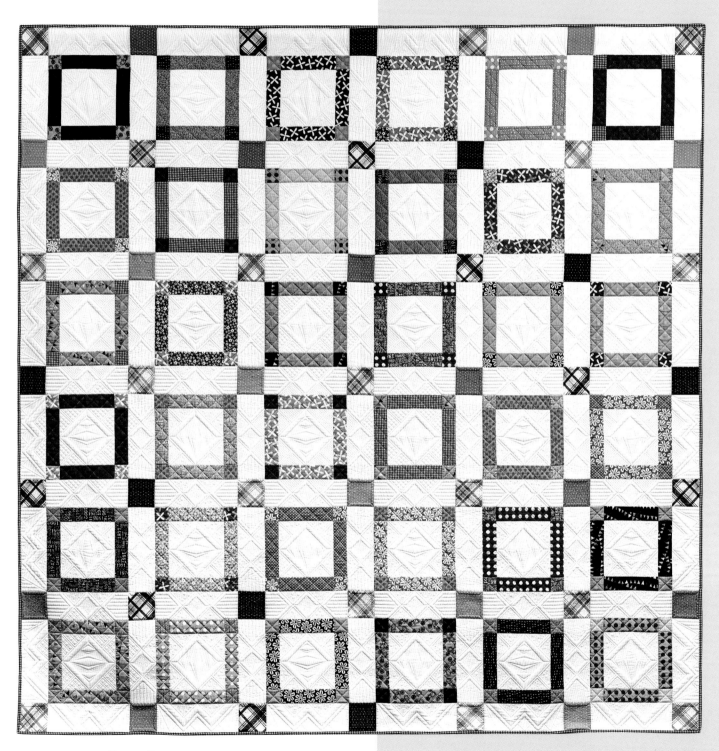

BIG BERTHA, 101" x 101"
Designed, pieced, and quilted by Judi Madsen

Big Bertha

Big Bertha was made using Moda Bella Solids fabric 9900-97 for the White fabric and fabric coordinating with Reunion by Sweetwater for Moda Fabrics. This quilt is organized, but is a perfect candidate for a scrappy quilt and a perfect stash buster.

I used two layers of 100% bleached cotton Hobbs batting and I used Fil-Tec Glide thread for the quilting, number 10002 Super White. I used Magna-Glide classic bobbins for the bobbin thread.

Fabric Requirements:

White Solid – 6 yards
Six (6) assorted fabric colors for sash squares
   – ⅙ yard each
A – Light Orange
B – Dark Orange
C – Light Blue
D – Dark Blue
E – Light Green
F – Aqua
9 assorted colors for blocks – ⅜ yard each
Binding – ⅞ yard
Backing – 3½ yards of 108" wide fabric
Batting – 3½ yards of 108" wide batting

Cutting
WHITE: SASHING AND CENTER OF BLOCKS

Cut ten (10) 12½" x WOF strips. Subcut rectangles measuring 12½" x 4½". You need a total of eighty-four (84) rectangles. You should be able to get nine (9) rectangles out of each strip, with six (6) left over.

Cut nine (9) 8½" x WOF strips. Subcut squares measuring 8½" x 8½". You need a total of thirty-six (36) squares and should be able to get four (4) squares from each strip with leftovers.

SASH SQUARES

A – Light Orange – Nine (9) 4½" squares
B – Dark Orange – Eight (8) 4½" squares
C – Light Blue – Eight (8) 4½" squares
D – Dark Blue – (Eight 8) 4½" squares
E – Light Green – Eight (8) 4½" squares
F – Aqua – Eight (8) 4½" squares

9 ASSORTED FABRIC COLORS FOR BLOCKS

Cut one (1) 8½" x WOF and one (1) 2½" x WOF strip from each of the 9 fabric colors.
    Subcut the 8½" strip into sixteen (16) rectangles measuring 2½" x 8½"
    Subcut the 2½" strip into sixteen (16) squares measuring 2½" x 2½"

BINDING

Cut twelve (12) 2½" x WOF strips

Block Assembly

You will need the following pieces to make thirty-six (36) blocks:

Thirty-six (36) White 8½" squares

(144) assorted 2½" x 8½" rectangles

(144) assorted 2½" squares

Each block will have two (2) differing colors for the squares and rectangles with one (1) White square in the middle as shown in the diagram (fig. 1).

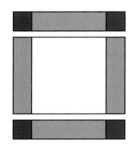

Fig. 1

1. Sew two (2) 2½" squares to each side of one (1) 2½" x 8½" rectangle to create a 2½" x 12½" section. Press seams down to stabilize stitches, then press seams toward the rectangle. Repeat this step to create two (2) sections per block.

2. Sew two (2) 2½" x 8½" rectangles to each side of one (1) 8½" square to create an 8½" x 12½" section. Press seams down, then press seams toward the rectangles.

3. Sew each row right sides together to create a 12½" x 12½" block. Press seams down, then press the seam away from the White square and toward the rectangle fabric. *Note:*

Pressing this way will make sure your quilting looks better in the White area! Always think ahead of your quilting when you are piecing your quilts.

Make a total of thirty-six (36) blocks.

Quilt Assembly

You will need the following to assemble the quilt top:

Thirty-six (36) quilt blocks

Eighty-four (84) 4½" x 12½" rectangles

Forty-nine (49) assorted A–F 4½" squares

This quilt will be sewn together in rows. There will be a total of seven (7) sash rows and six (6) block rows. Use the diagram (fig. 2, p. 60) for sash square and row placement. *Note: The block placement is up to you. Just have fun with it since this is a scrappy quilt!*

1. Sew each horizontal sash row together pressing each seam toward the squares.

2. Sew each block row together pressing each seam toward the blocks.

3. Finally, sew each sash row and block row together to finish the quilt top. Be sure to pin seam allowances to keep the points straight and crisp. Press seams toward the blocks. The goal is to minimize the seams showing on the White fabric. Try to press toward the darker fabric whenever possible.

Note: I find that when I am piecing a large

quilt top, it is easier for me to piece the rows in sections. Then sew the sections together. For example, on this quilt I would piece this quilt in three (3) sections, two (2) block rows each with sash rows in between. Once those three (3) sections are pieced, then I will sew them together. It is a lot easier than piecing row by row and will also give you a straighter quilt top.

Note: Piece the rows with the White rectangle strips on the top layer going through your machine. This will also help to keep your quilt from stretching and should give you a straighter result.

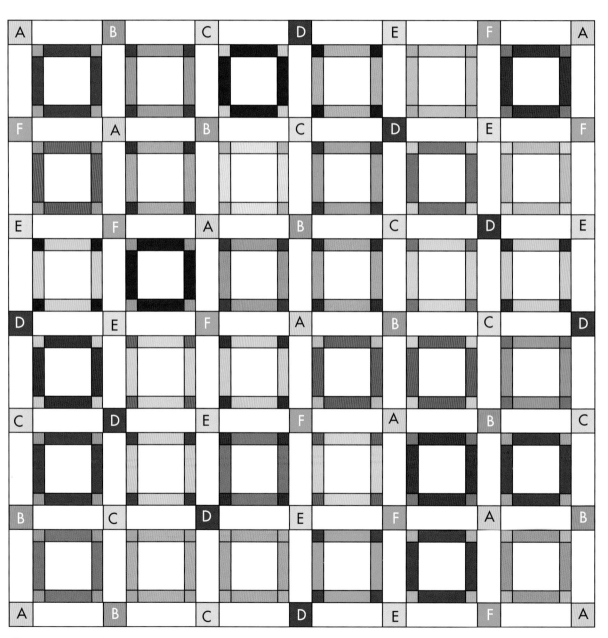

Fig. 2

Secondary **Designs** | Judi Madsen

Drawing the Designs and Quilting BIG BERTHA

Be aware that this quilt is big, really big! Most likely by the end of the quilt, you may be complaining about how long it has taken you. However, I promise you that when you pull this quilt off the frames, you are going to love it. I feel like if I don't hate a quilt by the time I have finished quilting it, I haven't put my whole heart into it. Seems kind of backwards, right? It works for me though.

There is a lot of drawing on this quilt. You will spend a lot of time drawing out the quilting designs. For this reason, I do not draw the designs on the entire quilt first, but rather draw only on the areas I am working on. It breaks up the monotony of this quilt.

You will stitch in the ditch this quilt to stabilize the areas that you are working on. With this quilt having a lot of vertical straight line seams, you will stitch in those seams first. I work from the center of the quilt out. Once the vertical seams are stitched, stitch in the ditch the horizontal seams. Stitching the seams in this order will help to keep your quilt straight and hopefully avoid puckers in the fabric. Since you will be using the same color thread throughout the quilt top, you will finish quilting an entire row before advancing your quilt.

Good luck and have fun!

Diagram Drawing and Quilting Diagram Instructions

DRAWING FOR SASH SQUARES 1A (fig. 3)

1. Draw a 3" square inside the 4" sash square. The lines will be ½" away from the edge of the sash square as shown in Orange.

2. Draw a small diagonal line in each corner from the small square to the outside of the sash square as shown in Red.

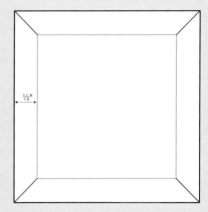

Fig. 3. Sash square 1A. Sash full size on the CD.

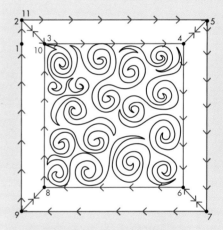

Fig. 4. Sash square 1B quilting path diagram. Diagram full size on the CD.

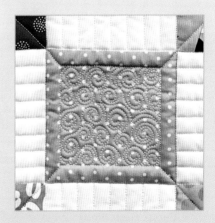

Fig. 5. Example showing a sash square

QUILTING PATH FOR SASH SQUARES 1B

1. In the top left corner of the outside of the sash square, put your needle down at point #1 and take a couple stitches, then quilt to the top left corner of the sash square. Continue to quilt around the outside of the square, stitching in the ditch and following the arrows shown in the diagram. Quilt all the way until you reach point #2 in the upper left corner, quilting over the stitches from point #1 and stop with the needle down (fig. 4, p. 61).

2. Quilt a straight diagonal line down until you reach point #3 which is the upper left corner of the drawn 3" square and continue to point #4, stop with needle down, then continue quilting diagonally up to point #5 and stop with the needle down.

3. Continue quilting diagonally down to point #4 traveling over your stitches, then continue to point #6 and stop with the needle down. Continue quilting from point #6 to point #7, then back to point #6 and continue on to point #8 and stop with the needle down.

4. Continue quilting to point #9 on the diagonal, then travel back on the stitches to point #8 and continue on to point #10 and stop with the needle down, this completes the inside square lines.

5. From point #10 free motion quilt a **Swirl** filler inside the 3" square. Quilt the **Swirls** with a motion around the block so that you can end up to point #10, then stop with the needle down. Continue quilting to point #11 traveling over your previous stitches. Take a couple of stay stitches, and cut your thread (fig. 5, p. 61).

DRAWING THE OUTSIDE SASH BORDER RECTANGLES 2A (fig.6)

1. Divide the 4" x 12" rectangle into (12) equal squares at 2" in (2) rows as shown in Purple. Make sure to measure from the inside of the rectangle to the outside. This will leave a ¼" space on the outside which will be your quilting reference line. The squares are labeled with letters for reference.

2. Draw one (1) line in each B, C, D, and E square to create two (2) triangles as shown in Blue.

3. Draw a line ¼" away and inside the two triangles drawn previously in step 2 as shown in Light Green.

4. Draw a diagonal line through squares A and K as shown in Pink. Continue line through square J, then square I, and finish through squares H and F as shown.

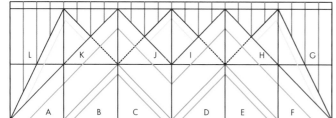

Fig. 6. Sash border 2A quilting path diagram. Diagram full size on the CD.

5. Draw a line ½" away and inside the lines previously drawn in step 4 (p. 62) as shown in Orange.

6. Draw a diagonal line within the squares A and L as shown in Pink. Continue the line from square L to halfway through square K, stopping at the line drawn in step 4. The black dotted lines show what point to use as a guideline to make it straight. In squares J and I, draw a line in each to create a square on point in the middle of the triangle from step 4. Finish drawing a line from the middle of H to the top of G and continue the line down to the bottom of F as shown in Pink.

7. Draw a line ¼" away and inside of each line previously drawn in step 6 as shown in Yellow.

8. Draw lines ½" apart on the outside of the sash design as shown in dark Green. There should be three (3) equal lines within each 2" area (fig. 7).

QUILTING PATH FOR OUTSIDE SASH BORDERS 2B (figs. 8 and 9, p. 64))

These instructions assume you will start and stop with the needle down and should be a continuous motion. You will travel over quilt lines. Also, you would have stitched in the ditch first to stabilize the area you are working on. Pay attention to the direction of the arrows to make quilting this sash block as easy as possible.

1. Start at point #1 and quilt the two inside triangle lines as shown in Green, stopping at point #2 with the needle down.

2. Continue quilting the inside filler circle/echo design within the two triangles and continue on to point #3.

3. Quilt the outside lines of the inside triangle as shown in Light Blue, continuing to point #4.

4. Continue quilting the inside large triangle straight lines as shown in Orange and continue to point #5.

5. Quilt the outside lines of the large triangle as shown in Red and stop at point #6.

6. Continue quilting the outside line of the square on point in the center of the design as shown in Pink, then continue quilting the inside line of the square on point until you quilt to point #7.

7. Fill the inside square on point with an up-and-down stitch filler, then continue to point #8.

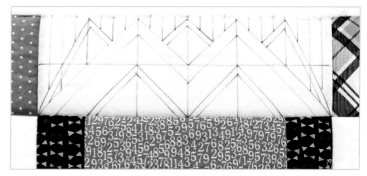

Fig. 7. Drawing of Section 2A

8. Quilting over your stitches, continue quilting the outside large triangle lines as shown in Aqua and continue to point #9.

9. Continue quilting the straight lines of the outside triangle design to point #12, down to #11. Finish quilting the inside straight lines as shown in Pink and stop at point #10.

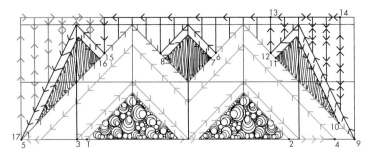

Fig. 8. Sash border 2B quilting path diagram. Diagram full size on the CD.

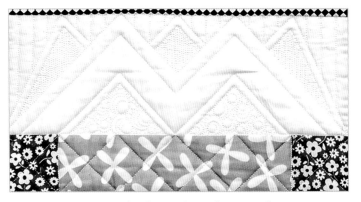

Fig. 9. Example of a Sash Border 2B quilting

10. Fill the inside area of the triangle with an up-and-down stitch as shown, continuing to point #11.

11. Take a small travel stitch to point #12.

12. Continue a straight stitch to point #13.

13. From this point stitch the ½" spaced lines in an up-and-down motion and continue to point #14.

14. Quilt a travel stitch from right to left at the top of the sash and continue until you get to the ½" spaced lines that have not been quilted. Quilt these lines from right to left in an up-and-down motion and continue until you get to point #15.

15. Continue quilting the outside straight lines as shown in Pink and continue to point #17. Then travel up to the inside straight lines and stitch until you get to point #16.

16. Quilt an up-and-down stitch to fill the inside of the triangle area, continuing to point #17.

17. Finish the design by quilting the remaining ½" spaced lines in an up-and-down motion as shown in Light Green.

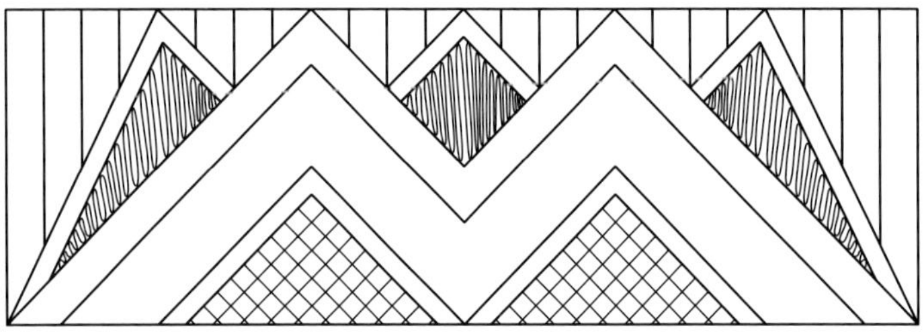

QUILTING PATH INSTRUCTIONS 2C

The instructions for this section are the same as 2B, except that step number 2 will be the ¼" straight line filler within the triangles as shown in the diagram (fig. 10).

Fig. 10. Sash border 2C quilting path diagram. Diagram full size on the CD.

Quilting Path Instructions 2D

The instructions for this section are the same as 2B, except that step number 2 will be the ½" straight line filler within the triangles as shown in figure 11.

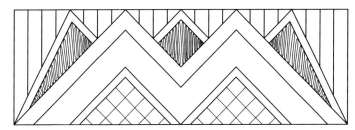

Fig. 11. Sash border 2D quilting path diagram. Diagram full size on the CD.

Quilting Path Instructions 2E

The instructions for this section are the same as 2B, except that step number 2 will be the ½" – ¼" straight line filler within the triangles as shown in figure 12.

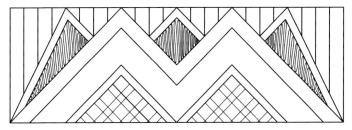

Fig. 12. Sash border 2E quilting path diagram. Diagram full size on the CD.

Drawing the Inside Sash Rectangles 3A (fig. 13, p. 66)

Please be aware that I will show you how to draw four (4) different fillers for these sash rectangles in this first diagram, but the actual quilting diagrams will be shown after the quilting path instructions for the sash rectangles.

1. Find the center of your sash rectangle at 6" and draw a line from this center line you will measure 4" out on both sides and draw a line as shown in Red. This will give you (3) reference lines.

2. Draw an X in between the center and outside lines as shown in Blue. This will give you (2) X's.

3. Ignoring the Red reference lines, you will draw a ½" line mimicking inside the end shapes on both sides of the rectangle as shown in Orange. Draw a line in the center of the shape previously drawn, then two more lines on each side of the center line at ½" increments.

For the center on-point square in the middle of the sash block, draw a ½" smaller on-point square, then draw lines from the smaller square points to the larger square points as shown in Orange.

4. Four (4) triangles were created when you drew the two (2) X's from step 2. Draw four (4) smaller triangles ¼" away from the outside edge of the triangle as shown in Green.

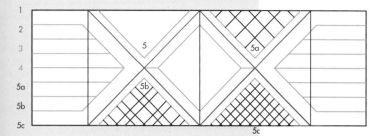

Fig. 13. Inside sash rectangles 3A quilting path diagram. Diagram full size on the CD.

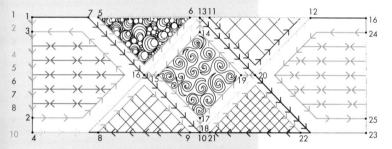

Fig. 14. Inside sash rectangles 3B quilting path diagram. Diagram full size on the CD.

*Filler options

5. Leave blank, this will be the free-motion circle/echo filler.

5a. Draw lines ½" apart.

5b. Draw lines ½", then ¼" apart as shown.

5c. Draw lines ¼" apart.

QUILTING PATH FOR THE INSIDE SASH RECTANGLES 3B (fig. 14)

These instructions assume you will start and stop with the needle down and should be a continuous motion. You will travel over quilt lines. Also, you would have stitched in the ditch first to stabilize the area you are working on. Pay attention to the direction of the arrows to make quilting this sash block as easy as possible. These instructions will also go over each filler design within one sash rectangle, but will be different when you quilt it. The diagrams for each sash rectangle quilting path designs are included at the end of these instructions as 3C, 3D, 3E, 3F, and 3G (figs. 15–20, p. 68).

1. Stitch a straight line from point #1 to point #2 as shown in Orange.

2. Stitch straight lines from point #2 to point #3 as shown in Orange.

3. Traveling along the ditch of the outside of the rectangle sash, stitch the ½" straight lines within the shape using an up-and-down or side-to-side motion, depending on if your sash is horizontal or vertical as shown in Blue. Stitch to point #4.

4. Stitch straight lines to point #5 as shown in Yellow.

5. Stitch inside triangle lines to point #6 as shown in Green.

6. Free motion quilt the circle/echo stitch, then continue to point #7.

7. Stitch straight lines to point #8 as shown in Red.

8. Stitch the inside triangle lines to point #9 as shown in Orange.

9. Stitch the inside straight lines for the filler design, then continue to travel back to point #10 as shown in Light Green.

10. Stitch straight lines to point #11 as shown in Yellow.

11. Stitch the inside triangle lines to point #12 as shown in Red.

12. Stitch the inside straight lines for the filler design, then continue to travel to point #13 as shown in Light Green.

13. From point #13, stitch down to point #14 as shown in Orange.

14. Stitch from point #14 to point #15 as shown in Orange.

15. Stitch from point #15 to point #16, then travel back on the same stitch line to point #15 as shown in Orange.

16. Stitch from point #15 to point #17 as shown in Orange.

17. Stitch from point #17 to point #18, then travel back on the same stitch line to point #17 as shown in Orange.

18. Stitch from point #17 to point #19 as shown in Orange.

19. Stitch from point #19 to point #20, then travel back on the same stitch line to point #19 as shown in Orange.

20. Stitch from point #20 to point #14. This will complete the inside on-point square. From this point quilt a **Swirl** filler design within the square and come back to point #14. Then continue on the same stitch line back to point #13 as shown in Orange.

21. Stitch straight lines from point #13 to point #21 as shown in Purple.

22. Stitch the straight lines of the inside triangle shape to point #22 as shown in Orange.

23. Stitch the inside straight filler design as shown in Light Green, then continue onto point #23 as shown in Light Green.

Fig. 15. Inside sash rectangles 3C quilting path diagram. Diagram full size on the CD.

Fig. 16. Inside sash rectangles 3D quilting path diagram. Diagram full size on the CD.

Fig. 17. Inside sash rectangles 3E quilting path diagram. Diagram full size on the CD.

Fig. 19. Inside sash rectangles 3G quilting path diagram. Diagram full size on the CD.

24. Use the ditch to stitch a straight line to point #24 as shown in Yellow.

25. Stitch straight lines to point #25 as shown in Orange.

26. Traveling along the ditch of the outside of the rectangle sash, stitch the ½" straight lines within the shape using an up-and-down or side-to-side motion, depending on if your sash is horizontal or vertical as shown in Aqua. Stitch to point #26 to finish.

Fig. 18. Inside sash rectangles 3F quilting path diagram. Diagram full size on the CD.

Fig. 20. Example of sash rectangle quilting

DRAWING REFERENCE AND QUILTING LINES FOR THE BLOCK 4A (fig. 21)

Keep in mind that I will have four (4) different filler designs within the block drawing, but the actual quilt block design you quilt will have only one (1) of the fillers. Pay attention to the layout and filler designs as you quilt the entire quilt.

1. Draw a line for each 2" section within the 2" x 8" rectangle as shown in Red. You should have three (3) lines in each rectangle. The remaining reference lines will be the square block seam allowances in the corners.

2. In the center 8" white square, draw four (4) lines to create an on-point square as shown in Orange.

3. From the on-point square, come in ¾" and draw a smaller square as shown in Yellow. Also, draw a small line from each corner of the square to the outside corner square as shown.

4. In each corner of the 8" square you should have a triangle. Draw a line in the center of that triangle as shown in Green.

5. With the line drawn in the previous step, you should now have two (2) triangles in each corner of the 8" square. Draw a smaller triangle in each section, ¼" away from previous lines as shown in Blue.

6. Using the top and bottom corners of the smaller on-point square as well as the corners of the outside triangles, draw a total of four

(4) lines to create two (2) V's inside the small square, as shown in Purple.

7. Draw a center horizontal line in the on-point square as shown in Red. Draw two (2) reference points per diamond section. The outer diamonds will have a reference point at ½" as well as ¼". The inner diamond shape will have two reference points at ½". Use the diagram for reference.

8. Draw ½" lines within the small triangle for filler design as shown in Orange.

9. Draw ½", then ¼" lines within the small triangle for filler design as shown in Yellow.

10. Draw ½" lines within the small triangle for filler design as shown in Green.

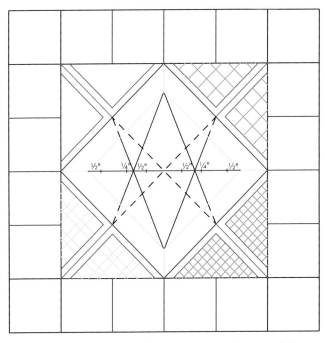

Fig. 21. Block 4A quilting lines diagram. Diagram full size on the CD.

QUILTING PATH FOR QUILT BLOCK 4B (fig. 22)

These instructions assume you stop with the needle down, travel over some previous stitches, and have already stitched in the ditch the outside of the block. Follow the arrows in the diagram for best results. The quilting path instructions will show the four (4) different filler options, however you will keep the filler designs consistent within each block. Examples of these are at the end of the quilting instructions as 4C, 4D, 4E, and 4F (figs. 23 – 26, pp. 73–74).

1. Start stitching at point #1 in the lower left corner of the block. Stitch diagonal straight lines from corner to corner of the 2" sections in the outside border of the block as shown in red. Stitch until point #2.

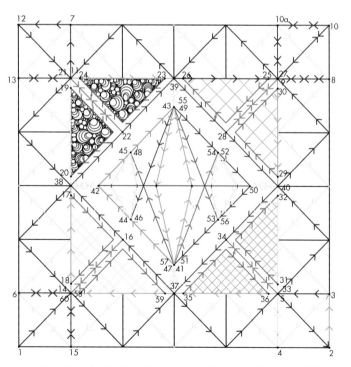

Fig. 22. Block 4B quilting path diagram. Diagram full size on the CD.

2. Stitch a straight line up to point #3 as shown in Orange.

3. Stitch a diagonal straight line down and to the left to point #4 as shown in Yellow.

4. Stitch up to point #5 in the ditch as shown in Yellow.

5. Travel over your stitch back down to point #4 as shown in Yellow.

6. Stitch diagonal straight lines up and down to point #6 as shown in Yellow.

7. Continue stitching straight diagonal lines up through the left side of the block as shown in Yellow and stitch to point #7.

8. Continue stitching straight diagonal lines up and down through the top of the block as shown in Yellow and stitch to point #8.

9. Continue stitching straight diagonal lines side to side and down to point #3 as shown in Yellow. Stitch in the ditch to the left along the top of the square to point #5 as shown in Red. Continue stitching diagonal lines side to side and up to point #9 as shown in Red.

10. Stitch a diagonal line up to point #10, then travel back on the stitch to point #9. Stitch a straight line up to point #10a and back down to point #9 as shown in Red.

11. Stitch diagonal straight lines right to left until point #11 as shown in Red.

12. Stitch in the ditch up to point #7, and continue with a right-to-left straight stitch to point #12 as shown in Red.

13. Stitch a diagonal straight line down to point #11, then continue the stitch in the ditch to point #13 as shown in Red.

14. Travel back on your stitch left to right to point #11. Continue stitching diagonal lines side to side and down to point #14 as shown in Red.

15. Stitch in the ditch a straight line down to point #15 and travel back up to point #14 as shown in Red.

16. Stitch in the ditch a straight line to the left to point #6 and travel back on the stitch to point #14 as shown in Red. Continue stitching a straight diagonal line up and to the right inside the white fabric to point #16. Travel back on this stitch to point #14 as shown in Green.

17. Stitch in the ditch up to point #17 as shown in Orange.

18. Stitch the inside triangle straight lines to point #18 as shown in Aqua.

19. Stitch the inside filler design (4F), in this case the ½" and ¼" lines as shown in Yellow, then continue stitching in the ditch up to point #19.

20. Stich the inside triangle straight lines to point #20 as shown in Aqua.

21. Stitch the inside filler design, in this case the free-motion circle/echo (4C), then continue stitching to point #21.

22. Stitch a diagonal line down and to the right to point #22 as shown in Green.

23. Travel back on this stitch up to point #21 as shown in Green.

24. Stitch in the ditch a straight line to the right to point #23 as shown in Orange.

25. Stitch the inside triangle straight lines to point #24 as shown in Aqua.

26. Stitch the inside triangle filler design, then continue on to point #25 as shown in Purple.

27. Stitch the inside triangle straight lines to point #26 as shown in Aqua.

28. Stitch the inside triangle filler design (4E), in this case the ½" lines as shown in Yellow, then continue to point #27.

29. Stitch a diagonal straight line down and to the left to point #28 as shown in Green.

30. Travel back on the straight diagonal stitch up to point #27 as shown in Green, then continue by stitching in the ditch down to point #29 as shown in Orange.

31. Stitch the inside triangle straight lines to point #30 as shown in Aqua.

32. Stitch the inside triangle filler design, then continue to stitch in the ditch to point #31 as shown in Yellow.

33. Stitch the inside triangle straight lines to point #32 as shown in Aqua.

34. Stitch the inside triangle filler design, in this case the ¼" straight lines (4D) as shown in Orange, then continue on to point #33.

35. Stitch a diagonal straight line up and to the left to point #34 as shown in Green.

36. Travel back down on stitch to get to point #33 as shown in Green, then continue to stitch in the ditch to point #35 as shown in Orange.

37. Stitch the straight lines for the inside triangle to point #36 as shown in Aqua.

38. Stitch the filler design inside the triangle design as shown in Orange, then continue stitching to point #37 as shown in Orange.

39. Stitch the outside diagonal line of the large on-point square up and to the left to point #38 as shown in pink.

40. Stitch a diagonal straight line up and to the right to point #39 as shown in pink.

41. Stitch a diagonal straight line down and to the right to point #40 as shown in pink.

42. Stitch a diagonal straight line down and to the left to point #37 to complete the on-point large square as shown in pink. Continue with a straight stitch up to point #41 as shown in pink.

43. Stitch a diagonal straight line up and to the left to point #42 as shown in Aqua. Stitch a straight line to the left to point #38, then travel back on the stitch to point #42.

44. Stitch a diagonal straight line up and to the right to point #43 as shown in Aqua. Stitch a straight line up to point #39, then travel back on the stitch to point #43.

45. Stitch a straight diagonal line down and to the left to point #44 as shown in pink.

46. Stitch two (2) straight lines to create the inside diamond shape, using the reference point as a guide, and stitch to point #45 as shown in Yellow.

47. Complete the diamond shape with two straight lines using the reference point down to point #46 as shown in Yellow.

48. Free motion stitch an up-and-down stitch to point #47 as shown in the diagram.

49. Stitch a straight diagonal line up and to the left to point #48 as shown in Blue.

50. Free motion stitch an up-and-down stitch to point #49 as shown in the diagram. Stitch the inside center diamond lines using the reference lines as shown in Orange. You will stitch from point #49 to point #47 and then back to point #49.

51. Stitch a straight diagonal line down and to the right to point #50 as shown in pink.

52. Stitch a straight diagonal line down and to the left to point #51 as shown in pink.

53. Stitch a straight diagonal line up and to the right to point #52 as shown in Aqua.

54. Stitch two (2) straight lines to create the inside diamond shape using the reference point as a guide and stitch to point #53 as shown in Yellow.

55. Complete the diamond shape with two straight lines using the reference point as a guide and stitch to point #54 as shown in Yellow.

56. Free motion stitch an up-and-down stitch up to point #55 as shown in the diagram.

57. Stitch a straight diagonal line down and to the right to point #56 as shown in Blue.

58. Free motion stitch an up-and-down stitch to point #57. Continue straight stitch traveling over the previous stitches down to point #37 as shown in Green.

59. Stitch in the ditch a straight line to the left to point #58 as shown in Green.

60. Stitch the inside triangle straight lines to point #59 as shown in Aqua.

61. Stitch the inside triangle filler design and then continue to point #60 and done!

Fig. 23. Block 4C quilting path diagram. Diagram full size on the CD.

Fig. 24. Block 4D quilting path diagram. Diagram full size on the CD.

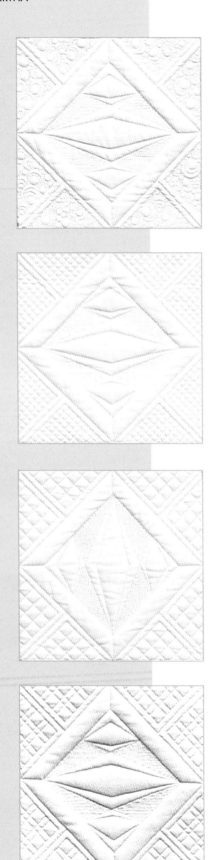

Fig. 25. Block 4E quilting path diagram. Diagram full size on the CD.

Fig. 26. Block 4F quilting path diagram. Diagram full size on the CD.

Secondary **Designs** I Judi Madsen

Now that we have all the drawing and quilting paths figured out, here is a layout for the quilting designs (fig. 27).

Fig. 27. Quilting placement

NORTH STAR, 81" x 81"
Designed, pieced, and quilted by Judi Madsen

NORTH STAR

NORTH STAR STATS

* Moda Bella Solids White 9900-97
* Print fabric from Reunion by Sweetwater for Moda Fabrics
* 2 layers Hobbs bleached White 100% cotton
* So Fine thread #401 by Superior Threads

Fabric Requirements

White – 7½ yards *(includes seamless borders)*
Blue – 1½ yards
Red – 1½ yards
Binding – ¾ yard
Backing – 5½ yards (45 WOF)
Batting – 90" square
Finished quilt approximately 81" x 81"

Cutting

WHITE

Cut six (6) 9½" x WOF strips
    Subcut twenty-four (24) 9½" squares
Cut ten (10) 7½" x WOF strips
    Subcut forty-eight (48) 7½" squares
Cut four (4) 8½" x WOF strips
    Subcut thirty-two (32) 8½" x 4½"
        rectangles

Cut three (3) 3½" x WOF strips
    Subcut thirty-two (32) 3½" squares
Cut two (2) border strips 8½" x 70" and set aside.
Cut two (2) border strips 8½" x 90" and set aside.

BLUE

Cut three (3) 9½" x WOF strips
    Subcut twelve (12) 9½" squares.
Cut two (2) 2½" x WOF strips
    Subcut twenty-four (24) 2½" squares
Cut two (2) 4½" x WOF strips
    Subcut sixteen (16) 4½" squares
Cut one (1) 1½" x WOF strip
    Subcut sixteen (16) 1½" squares

RED

Cut three (3) 9½" x WOF strips
    Subcut twelve (12) 9½" squares
Cut two (2) 2½" x WOF strips
    Subcut twenty-four (24) 2½" squares
Cut two (2) 4½" x WOF strips
    Subcut sixteen (16) 4½" squares
Cut one (1) 1½" x WOF strip
    Subcut sixteen (16) 1½" squares

BINDING

Cut nine (9) strips 2½" x WOF and set aside.

Let's get started!

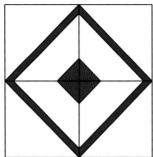

Fig. 1. Large Diamond block

Large Diamond Blocks (fig. 1)

You will make six (6) Blue Diamond blocks and six (6) Red Diamond blocks. You will need the following to make twelve (12) blocks:

Twenty-four (24) White 9½" squares
Forty-eight (48) White 7½" squares
Twelve (12) Blue 9½" squares
Twelve (12) Red 9½" squares
Twenty-four (24)Blue 2½" squares
Twenty-four (24) Red 2½" squares

Fig. 2   Fig. 3

HALF-SQUARE TRIANGLES (HSTs)

1. Draw a diagonal line from corner to corner on the White 9½" squares.

2. Place a White 9½" square right sides together with a Blue 9½" square and sew ¼" away from and on both sides of the line drawn (fig. 2).

Fig. 4   Fig. 5

3. Cut along the drawn line to get two (2) HSTs (fig. 3). Press the seam toward Blue in one (1) HST and press the seam toward White in the other HST.

4. Trim the HSTs to an 8½" square.

5. Draw a diagonal line from corner to corner on the White 7½" squares.

Fig. 6   Fig. 7

6. Place a White 7½" square right sides together in the corner of the Blue fabric as shown in figure 4. Sew along the drawn line.

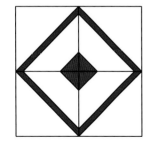

Fig. 8

7. Trim excess fabric, leaving a ¼" seam allowance and press the seams (fig. 5, p. 78).

Note: This block consists of four (4) squares sewn together. The seams within the block will be pressed opposite of the other seams. Half the block will be pressed toward the White fabric, half toward the color fabric. Just make sure you pay attention to that as you piece and assemble each block.

8. Draw a diagonal line from corner to corner on the wrong side of the Red fabric 2½" squares.

9. Place a Red 2½" square right sides together in the corner of the White 7½" fabric square as shown in figure 6, page 78. Sew along the drawn line.

10. Trim excess fabric, leaving a ¼" seam allowance and press the seam (fig. 7, p. 78).

You will need to make four (4) of these squares per large Diamond block. You will need twenty-four (24) squares to make six (6) large Diamond blocks in this color combination. Then, repeat steps 1–10 with the Red 9½" squares and the Blue 2½" squares. Make six (6) large Diamond blocks as well (fig. 8, p. 78).

Small Diamond Blocks (fig. 9)

You will make four (4) Red Diamond blocks and four (4) Blue Diamond blocks. You will need the following to make eight (8) blocks:

Thirty-two (32) White 8½" x 4½" rectangles
Thirty-two (32) White 3½" squares
Sixteen (16) Red 4½" squares
Sixteen (16) Blue 4½" squares
Sixteen (16) Red 1½" squares
Sixteen (16) Blue 1½" squares

1. Draw a diagonal line from corner to corner on the wrong side of two (2) Red 4½" squares. Place the squares on the right side of two (2) White 8½" x 4½" rectangles.

2. Sew along the diagonal lines, but pay attention to line placement in figure 10 on page 80, because each rectangle will be different.

3. Trim the excess fabric, leaving a ¼" seam allowance and press the seams. Press the seam in one rectangle to the White fabric and press the seam in the other rectangle to the Red fabric (fig. 11, p. 80).

4. Draw a diagonal line from corner to corner on the wrong side of two (2) White 3½" squares. Place the White squares right sides

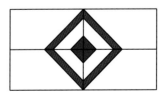

Fig. 9. Small Diamond block

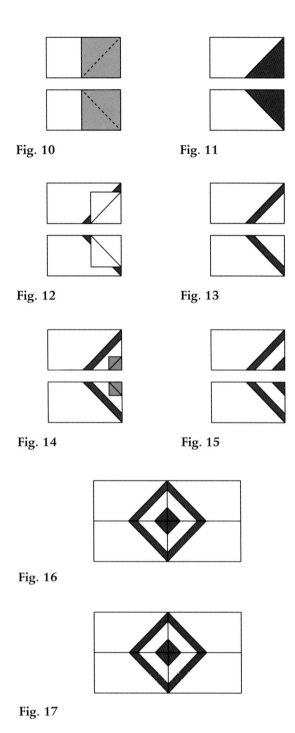

Fig. 10

Fig. 11

Fig. 12

Fig. 13

Fig. 14

Fig. 15

Fig. 16

Fig. 17

together on the Red fabric side of the 8½" x 4½" rectangles and sew along the drawn line (fig. 12).

5.   Trim excess fabric, leaving a ¼" seam allowance and press seams (fig. 13).

6.   Draw a diagonal line from corner to corner on the wrong side of two (2) Blue 1½" squares. Place the Blue squares right sides together on the White fabric side of the 8½" x 4½" rectangles and sew along the drawn lines (fig. 14).

7.   Trim excess fabric, leaving a ¼" seam allowance and press the seams (fig. 15).

8.   Repeat steps 1–7 for the other side of the block. Then sew the four (4) sections together using a ¼" seam allowance to make one (1) small Diamond block. Make four (4) blocks (fig. 16).

Use the instructions above to make four (4) Blue small Diamond blocks using the Blue 4½" squares and the Red 1½" squares with the White 8½" x 4½" rectangles (fig. 17).

Block Layout and Final Assembly

You will need the following to complete the quilt top center.

Six (6) Blue large Diamond blocks
Six (6) Red large Diamond blocks
Four (4) Blue small Diamond blocks
Four (4) Red small Diamond blocks

1. Sew the blocks together using a ¼" seam allowance into four (4) rows. Follow figure 18 for block placement.

2. Sew the rows together, be sure to pin seam allowances, and press seams well.

3. Measure the vertical length of the quilt through the center and trim the 2 side border strips to this measurement. Sew them to the sides of the quilt. Press seams toward the border.

4. Measure the width of the quilt through the center, including the side borders you just added. Trim the remaining 2 border strips to this measurement and sew them to the top and bottom of the quilt according to the quilt assembly figure below.

Congrats on finishing the quilt top! Now on to the quilting!

Fig. 18. Block layout

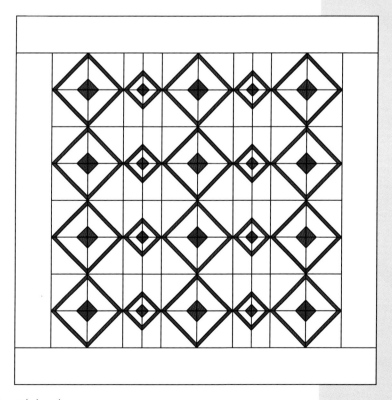

Fig. 19. Quilt assembly with borders

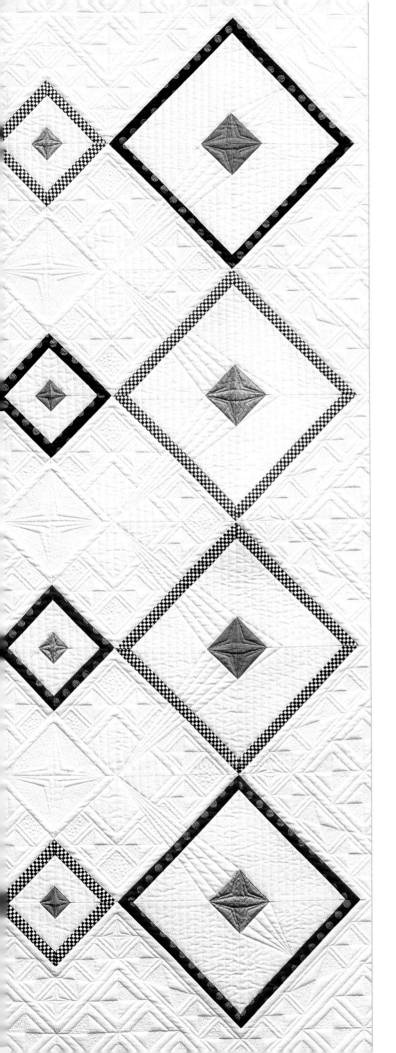

North Star – The Quilting!

This quilt is amazing, and I had a wonderful time working on it. The simple diamond square design concept with the enormous amount of white fabric provided the perfect background for this intense quilting. This quilt was not hard to quilt, but it was a little more time consuming making sure that the tiling square backgrounds were even and straight. I will have you know that my quilting is not perfect. Some of the squares are a bit larger, and some are a bit smaller. The time I took to divide the space and draw as I worked on the quilt allowed it to come out looking pretty consistent. I will be showing you what lines in the quilting designs to draw first so that your quilt will be as even as possible. Also, it helps to have a straight quilt, so be sure to piece using quality fabric. No pressure!

I hope that this quilt top and its quilting does not intimidate you, but gives you the drive to try something new. The tiling effect in the quilting design is one of my favorite secondary designs. I have used this design before on some of my quilts for clients, but this is the first time I have used it as a specific border design that was inspired by the piecing design. The pieced top and the quilting were meant to be together, and I hope you can see that in the design.

The quilting in this quilt can be drawn while on the quilting frames. I did not pre-draw anything for this quilt top, but that would be different if you were quilting on a domestic machine. So plan accordingly. I have 50–60 hours of drawing and quilting put into this quilt top, so be ready for long hours. Also, the instructions for this quilt are not necessarily in quilting order. Please keep that in mind as you read through the instructions first. Let's get started!

FILLERS

This quilt top has 3 filler designs, **Pebbles** (fig. 20), **Swirls** (fig. 21), and **Side-to-Side** (fig. 22) stitches. I like to keep things simple.

Fig. 20. Pebbles

Fig. 21. Swirls

HOURGLASS SQUARE TILING

The hourglass square tiling blocks in the outside border background of the quilt top will be roughly 3⅜" squares (fig. 23). The size will depend on your quilt top but use the information below to draw the lines needed in each square. The instructions on where the square will be will come later.

1. Draw an X inside each of the squares (fig. 24, p. 84).

2. Draw a smaller square within the bigger square ½" away from the outside lines.

Fig. 22. Side to side

Quilting

3. Start at point #1 and stitch straight lines to point #2, then to point #3, then to point #4, and finally to point #5. This completes the outside square.

4. Stitch a straight diagonal line from point #5 to point #6.

5. Traveling on the previous straight line, stitch from point #6 to point #7. Continue by stitching a diagonal line from point #7 to point #8, the inside square corner.

Fig. 23. Hourglass square tiling

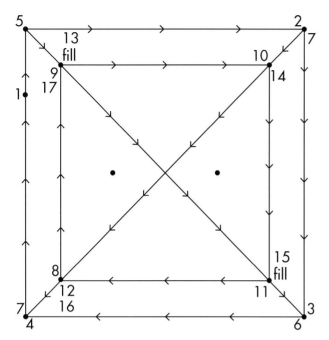

Fig. 24. Hourglass square tiling path diagram 1A. Diagram full size on the CD. Diagrams 1A through 5A shown on the same diagram on the CD.

6. Stitch the inside square straight lines from point #8 to point #9, then point #9 to point #10, then from point #10 to point #11. Then continue to point #12 completing the inside square design.

7. Fill in the side triangle with a free-motion swirl to point #13.

8. Stitch along the previous straight line from point #13 to point #14.

9. Fill in the other side triangle with a free-motion swirl to point #15.

10. Stitch a straight line traveling on the previous line from point #15 to point #16, then stitch a diagonal line from point #16 to point #17 to complete the square.

The quilting instructions for this block are written as a single block, but keep in mind that you will use previous stitching lines from tiling squares to travel on to get to the next block to stitch out the design.

INSIDE BORDER SQUARES AND RECTANGLES (fig. 25)

Fig. 25. Border squares and rectangles

1. Draw an X through the 2" square as shown in Red (fig. 26).

2. Draw a smaller square inside the larger square ¼" away from the outside lines as shown in Orange.

3. Draw a small dot on the right and left triangles within the design. These triangles will be stitched with the **Swirl** filler.

The drawing instructions for the large (3A, fig. 27) and small rectangles (4A, fig. 28) in the border design are the same.

1. Draw a smaller rectangle ¼" away from the outside edges of the rectangle as shown in Orange.

2. Draw (2) lines to create an X in the smaller rectangle as shown in Red.

3. Draw a straight line from the corner of the small rectangle to the outside corner of the large rectangle. Draw a line for each corner of the rectangle as shown in Yellow.

4. Draw a dot for quilting reference on each side triangle as shown in Yellow. These triangles will be stitched with a **Swirl** filler.

The quilting instructions are the same as the large hourglass tiling square.

The 5A design will be in the corner of each point in the border design (fig. 29, p. 86). The drawing and quilting instructions are as follows:

Drawing

1. Draw an X in the square as shown in Red (fig. 30, p. 86).

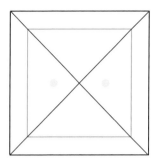 

Fig. 26. Square 2A

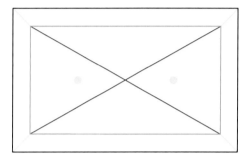

Fig. 27. Large rectangle 3A

Fig. 28. Small rectangle 4A

Diagrams 1A through 5A shown on the same diagram on the CD.

Fig. 29. Border corner design 5A

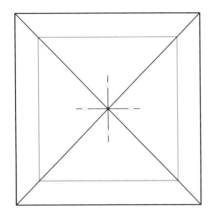

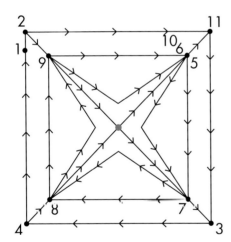

Fig. 30. Border corner design 5A diagram

Diagrams 1A through 5A shown on the same diagram on the CD.

2. Draw a smaller square inside the larger square ¼" away from the outside as shown in Orange.

3. In the middle of the X, draw two perpendicular lines, one horizontal and one vertical line as shown in Black.

4. Draw a reference point along the perpendicular lines ¼" away from the center of the X as shown in Yellow.

Quilting

1. Start stitching at point #1, quilting all 4 of the outside lines in the square and continue to point #2.

2. Continue stitching from point #2 with a diagonal straight line down to point #3.

3. Travel over previous stitches from point #3 to point # 4.

4. Continue stitching from point #4 to the corner of the inside square at point #5.

5. Stitch the (4) inside lines of the smaller square, continuing to point #6.

6. Following the arrows stitch the inside triangle lines, quilting to the Green center reference point to point #7.

7. Continue from point #7 to point #8, then from point #8 to point #9, then from point #9 to point #10.

8. Stitch the last corner from point #10 to point #11.

DRAWING 9A AND 9B

The instructions for marking the following designs are separated into sections. Please use figure 31 for placement. I will start with diagram 9A (fig. 32) so that the remaining sections will make sense as you draw them.

The drawing in this section should not be too difficult, but will take some time. I used the seam allowances to help with line placement. To avoid mistakes, look twice, mark once. In the center of the diagram are four (4) points, A and B are on the horizontal line and C and D are on the vertical line.

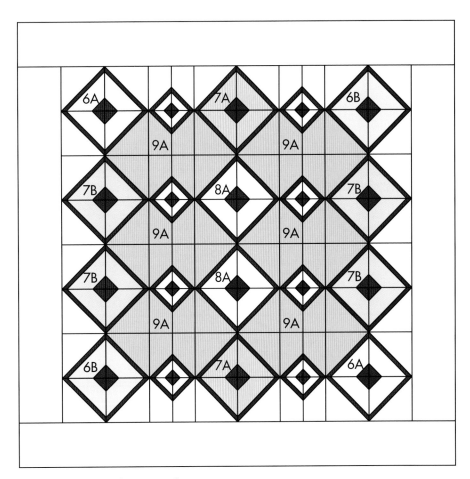

Fig. 31. Quilting placement diagram

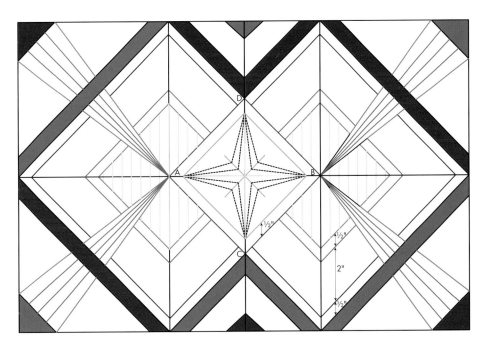

Fig. 32. Section 9A quilting path diagram. Diagram full size on the CD.

1. In the center part of this design, draw four (4) straight diagonal lines to make an on-point square. Connect the A, B, C, and D points as shown in Red.

2. Draw a smaller on-point square ½" inside the large square from step #1 as shown in Orange. Now draw an X as a reference quilting line in the center of the smaller square as shown in Orange. Now draw two (2) reference points ½" and 1" from the center seam on each side of the X as shown in Orange.

3. Draw straight diagonal lines from each corner of the smaller on-point square to the center reference points drawn in step #2 as shown in Yellow.

4. Draw the two (2) outside lines of the long triangle shapes that continue beyond the

piecing as shown in Green. The lines come out from points A and B, continuing to the outside edge of the pieced Red and Blue triangles in the corner of the diagram or the pieced center of the Diamond blocks. There are four (4) large triangles, two (2) on each side.

5. Draw three (3) equal lines between the two (2) Green lines just drawn. Draw the center line first then draw a line on both sides of that line to keep it even. The lines are shown in Blue.

6. Draw straight lines ½" away from the Red and Blue pieced fabric to mimic the shape in the White area. Do not draw in the center on-point square. This shape and its lines are shown in Purple.

7. Come in 2" from the Purple line and draw one partial on-point square on both sides of the center on-point square as shown in Blue. Do not draw through the Green and Blue lines from the large triangle shape drawn in steps 4 and 5.

8. Come in ½" from the Blue lines on the partial on-point squares and draw a smaller on-point square inside the larger squares as shown in Green.

9. Use the vertical center seam allowance as a guide to draw ½" spaced vertical lines in each partial on-point square as shown in Yellow.

That completes the drawing for 9A (fig. 33). This could be a fabulous quilt design by itself, but we always love adding detail, right?

Fig. 33. Section 9A

Fig. 34. Section 9B quilting path diagram. Diagram full size on the CD.

Continuing: Section 9B (fig. 34)

10. In between the Blue 2" spaced lines draw two (2) lines to make a 2" square in each corner of the design as shown in Red. There are six (6) corners, so draw six (6) squares.

11. Draw a line to make another 2" square on each side of the six (6) corner squares as shown in Yellow. This will give you three (3) equal squares in each of the six (6) corners of the design. The remaining areas will be irregular rectangles.

12. Draw a smaller square ¼" inside each of the corner 2" squares as shown in Yellow. Draw three (3) straight lines ¼" inside the irregular rectangles mimicking the shape as shown in Yellow. Quilt the **Pebble** filler inside the Yellow lines.

13. In the remaining corner squares draw an X inside the square as shown in Green.

14. Draw a smaller square ¼" inside the remaining squares as shown in Blue.

15. Draw a dot in two (2) of the triangles inside each of the squares as shown in Purple. This dot will help you to know to quilt the **Swirl** filler when you are quilting this design.

The photo (fig. 35, p. 90) shows you how one side of 9AB will look when it is drawn on the quilt top.

The quilting path for this particular design can be what you want it to be. However, to keep the quilt as straight as possible and to avoid puckering in your quilt, it is best to have the large triangle lines and the center on-point square

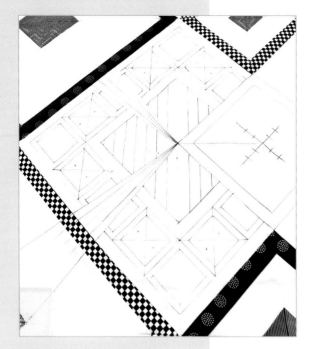

Fig. 35. Section 9AB drawn on quilt top

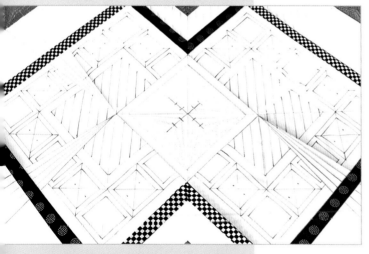

Fig. 36. Section 9AB quilted first to stabilize

quilted or stabilized first. You can see that I have quilted these elements first in the photo (fig. 36). You will also want to stabilize the quilting by stitching in the ditch. Once you have quilted the stabilizing elements of the design, continue quilting each section of the design.

DRAWING INSTRUCTIONS FOR 6A (fig. 37, p. 91) AND 6B (fig. 38, p. 91)

1. Use the center seam allowance in the middle of the small pieced on-point square and the outside seam allowance to draw a diagonal line in the center of the large on-point block as shown in Red.

2. Draw two (2) lines to create a triangle in the top corner of the large on-point square using the centerline and edges of the small pieced on-point square for reference. The opposite side of the triangle point design should have already been drawn from diagram 9A. However, the design lines are drawn here for reference and are shown in Orange.

3. Draw two (2) more lines in between and equal distance from the Red and Orange lines as shown in Yellow.

4. Using the vertical center seam allowance for reference, draw ½" spaced lines to fill in the remaining area of the large on-point square as shown in Green.

The instructions for 6B are the same as 6A, only the lines are mirrored. Be sure to use the diagram for reference and placement on the quilt.

DRAWING INSTRUCTIONS FOR 7A (fig. 39)

1. Draw the outside diagonal lines, if you have not already, using the center on-point square and outside seam allowance for reference, shown in Red. Draw a reference point 1" from the top of the small on-point square as shown in Red.

2. Draw two (2) lines connecting the on-point square to the center reference point as shown in Orange.

Draw the remaining lines between the Red lines if you have not already done that.

3. Using the vertical center seam allowance for reference, draw ½" spaced lines to fill in the remaining area of the large on-point square as shown in Green.

DRAWING INSTRUCTIONS FOR 7B (fig. 40)

The instructions for 7B are similar to 7A. Just remember that the design is on the side, not the top like 7A. Use the diagram for reference.

To quilt sections 6A, 6B, 7A, and 7B, first stabilize the inside large on-point square with a stitch in the ditch, then quilt the triangle and diagonal straight lines. Finish by quilting the vertical straight lines.

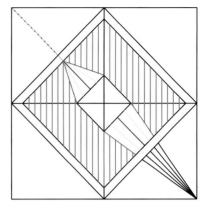

Fig. 37. Section 6A quilting path diagram. Diagram full size on the CD.

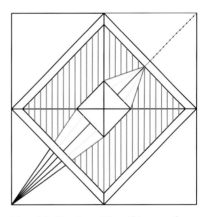

Fig. 38. Section 6B quilting path diagram. Diagram full size on the CD.

Fig. 39. Section 7A quilting path diagram. Diagram full size on the CD.

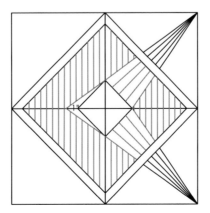

Fig. 40. Section 7B quilting path diagram. Diagram full size on the CD.

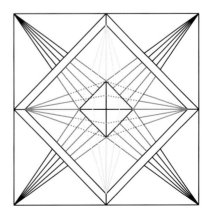

Fig. 41. Section 8A quilting path diagram. Diagram full size on teh CD.

DRAWING INSTRUCTIONS FOR 8A
(fig. 41, p. 91)

1. Draw five (5) evenly dispersed straight lines on each side of the on-point small pieced square as shown in Orange.

2. Use the small pieced on-point square and the top and bottom points of the large on-point square for reference and draw five (5) evenly dispersed lines in the background as shown in Yellow.

3. Use the small pieced on-point square and the side points of the large on-point square for reference and draw five (5) evenly dispersed lines in the background as shown in Green.

4. The remaining empty space will be quilted with a **Swirl** fill.

To quilt this section, first stabilize the inside large on-point square with a stitch in the ditch, then quilt the straight and diagonal lines. Finish by quilting the **Swirl** fill in the empty spaces.

You can figure the rest out on your own. Just kidding of course! But, if you made it this far, then we can talk about the borders. See, I told you this project would take forever—or maybe it is taking me forever to write about. I can't tell right now. It will be worth it though, I mean just look at this quilt border!

The Borders

The inside border design needs to be drawn first, making way for the tiling blocks in the outer border. The design follows the lines in the piecing along the Red and Blue fabric (fig. 42). The diagrams are progressive drawings that will eventually cover all the designs within the borders, but will not show the entire border. The rest of the borders will need to be drawn in as you advance the quilt and will use the same drawing methods shown in 10A and 10B (figs. 43-44, page 93), and 10C (fig. 46, p. 95). Use the diagrams for help as well as the photos from my own project to get the drawing just right.

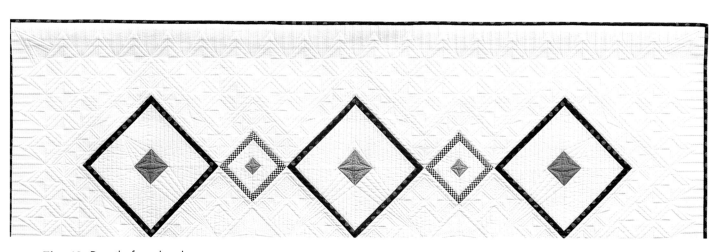

Fig. 42. Detail of top border

DRAWING INSTRUCTIONS FOR 10A

(fig. 43)

1. Draw straight lines following the piecing of the Red and Blue fabrics ½" away from the seam allowance as shown in Red.

2. Draw straight lines that mimic the previous lines 2" away from the Red lines as shown in Orange.

3. Draw straight lines that mimic the previous lines ½" away from the Orange lines as shown in Yellow.

These lines will continue all the way around the quilt. Use the outside lines to help draw the tiling squares in the borders. The following drawing instructions are for the top and bottom borders where the small on-point fabric squares are located.

4. Draw two (2) lines out to the edge of the quilt from point #1 to make a V as shown in Green. In the middle of point #1 and #3 draw a line in the center from point #2 to the outside edge of the quilt on both sides of the V as shown in Green.

5. Draw diagonal lines from point #4 to the outside edge of the quilt on both sides of the large on-point squares as shown in Blue. In between points #3 and #4 draw a diagonal line in the center from point #5 to the outside edge of the quilt as shown in Blue.

6. Draw diagonal lines from point #6 to the outside edge of the quilt in between points #3 and #5 as shown in Purple.

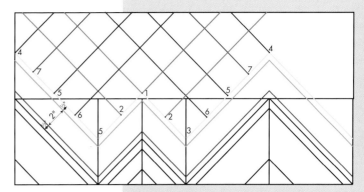

Fig. 43. Section 10A quilting path diagram. Diagram full size on the CD.

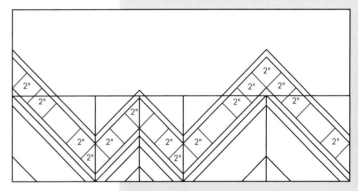

Fig. 44. Section 10B quilting path diagram. Diagram full size on the CD.

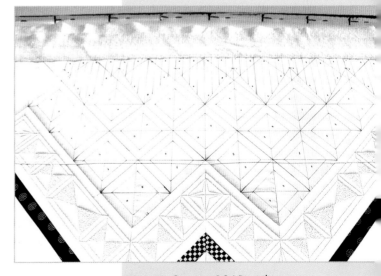

Fig. 45. Section 10AB quilting

This completes the outside lines for the tiling squares, but the final border design will be drawn a little later. Let's keep going.

DRAWING INSTRUCTIONS FOR 10B
(fig. 44, p. 93)

The lines drawn will be in between the 2" spaced lines drawn previously in 10A.

1. In each corner of the 2" spaced section draw two (2) lines to make a 2" square as shown in Red. The inside motif design in each one of these corner squares will be 5A (fig. 29, p. 86).

2. Use the Red lines as a reference to draw out more 2" squares as shown in Orange. The inside small section will only have one (1) extra 2" square on either side of the bottom 5A square with a small irregular rectangle in the upper corner. The large inside section will have two (2) squares on each side of the corner 5A square with one (1) large irregular rectangle in the middle as shown.

＊ The 2" squares on either side of the 5A corner squares will be drawn as motif 2A.

＊ The small and large irregular rectangle will be drawn as motifs 3A and 4A.

This would be a good time to quilt this part of the quilt.

First, stitch in the ditch to stabilize the seams in the quilt then work outward by stitching the straight lines that are ½" away from the seam allowance. Continuing stitching

the straight lines 2" from the previous line then fill in the square motifs. Finally, stitch the outside line that is ½" from the previous line, (fig. 45, p. 93).

DRAWING INSTRUCTIONS FOR 10C
(fig. 46, p. 95)

The following instructions will cover drawing for the remaining large areas on the sides of the quilt as well as in the corners. It will also go over the lines drawn to make the edge border design. You will need to find the center marks and measure to make sure your lines make squares that are straight. If you draw the lines in the order of the directions given, you should have straight squares.

1. Use the diagram for reference and draw lines from points #1 to the outside edge of the quilt as shown in Red. There is also a point #1 in the center of the corner section of the quilt. Draw a diagonal line from the center point #1 to the outside corner of the quilt as shown in Red.

2. Use the diagram for reference and draw lines by finding the center of points #1 and #4, starting at points #2 to the outside edge of the quilt as shown in Orange.

3. Use the diagram for reference and draw lines by finding the center of points #1 and #2 and #2 and #4, starting at points #3 to the outside edge of the quilt as shown in Yellow. You will also need to draw four (4) lines from point #3 to the outside edge of the quilt in the corner design as shown in Yellow.

4. Measure the squares that you have already drawn. The squares should be around 3⅜". Draw diagonal lines from point #5 to #5, then #6 to #6, and so on until #8 as shown in Green.

5. The top row of whole on-point squares will be the outside edge of the quilting design. Draw a line from the top of the square to the edge of the quilt as shown in Blue and as point #9. Along that line draw a reference point 1" from the top corner of the square as shown. Now, draw two (2) lines connecting the reference point and the sides of the on-point square as shown in Blue and in the photo (fig. 47).

6. Draw the X's in each square 3⅜" square.

CORNER DESIGN

1. Use the center point in the corner squares as a reference and draw a diagonal line 2" long to the center line of the quilt as shown in the photo (fig. 48, fig. 96). Draw a line on both sides of the line to make a triangle.

2. Draw two (2) lines ¼" away from the first triangle lines drawn in step 1. Draw two (2) more triangles, the first one ½" away from the previous line, the second one ¼" away from that line as shown in the photo (fig. 49, fig. 96).

3. Finish drawing the inside squares using

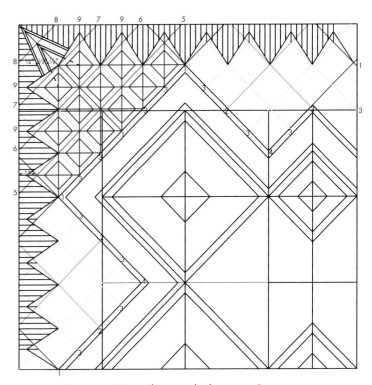

Fig. 46. Section 10C quilting path diagram. Diagram full size on the CD.

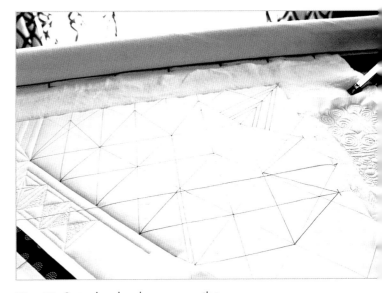

Fig. 47. Outer border drawn on quilt top

Fig. 48

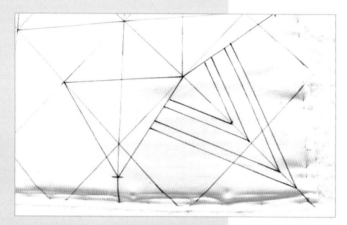

Fig. 49

the instructions for 1A, alternating the dots for the **Swirl** fill.

4. Draw the ½" spaced lines in the remaining area as shown in the photo (fig. 50). Draw a dot in every other line as a reference for the **Side-to-Side** fill design.

Now, go and quilt it! As you quilt, you will be able to come up with a quilting path that works for you. I typically start from the inside and work my way out to the edge of the quilt. In the photo above you can see how I work my way down the quilt in sections as I draw the design, stabilizing as I go. See the quilting detail of the back of NORTH STAR on p. 9.

Have fun with the quilting because it is going to be fabulous!

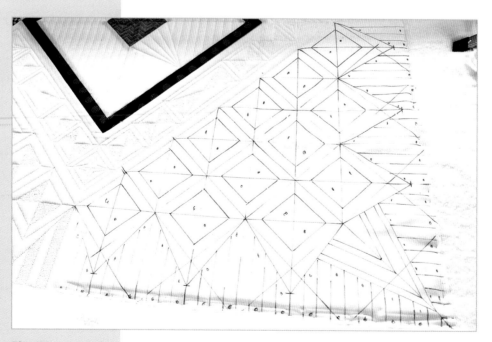

Fig. 50

PLAYTIME, 93" x 93"
Designed and quilted by Judi Madsen
Pieced by Thelma Childers

Playtime

Playtime Stats

* Moda Bella Solids Bleached White 9900-98 for the background fabric in the quilt top
* Batting: Two layers of 100% bleached cotton Hobbs Heirloom
* Thread: Fil-Tec Glide Super White 10002 for top, Magna-Glide bobbins for the bottom

I pulled the Dark Plum solid and Dark Celery Green fabrics from my stash for the inspiration of the colors in this quilt top. The other colors are a result of trial and error and buying way too much fabric at my local quilt shops. I tried out several color combinations of fabrics before I came up with my final fabric pull. I think this is my favorite color combination I have ever used on a quilt.

Fabric Requirements

White – 7¾ yards (includes enough for seamless border strips)
Dark Plum (color 1) – ⅔ yard
Light Plum (color 2) – ¾ yard
Light Aqua (color 3) – ½ yard
Fuchsia (color 4) – ⅔ yard
Dark Aqua (color 5) – ⅔ yard
Dark Green (color 6) – ⅔ yard
Black (color 7) – ½ yard
Light Green (color 8) – ½ yard

Binding – ⅞ yard
Backing – 9 yards of 44" fabric pieced in three (3) equal three (3) yard pieces, or three (3) yards of 108" fabric
Batting – 108" x 108"

Cutting

WHITE

Cut four (4) 12½" x WOF strips
  Subcut twenty (20) 6½" x 12½" rectangles
Cut nine (9) 6½" x WOF strips
  Subcut fifty-two (52) 6½" squares
Cut three (3) 6½" x WOF strips
  Subcut thirty-two (32) 3½" x 6½" rectangles
Cut four (4) 3½" x WOF strips
  Subcut seventy-two (72) 2" x 3½" rectangles

Cut two (2) 3½" x WOF strips
Subcut sixteen (16) 3½" squares
Cut two (2) 2" x WOF strips and set aside for
strip piecing
Cut two (2) border strips 7" x 84" and set
aside
Cut two (2) border strips 7" x 96" and set
aside

DARK PLUM (COLOR 1)
Cut two (2) 4½" x WOF strips
Subcut sixteen (16) 4½" squares
Cut two (2) 3½" x WOF strips
Subcut twenty-four (24) 3½" squares

LIGHT PLUM (COLOR 2):
Cut (2) 4½" x WOF strips
Subcut (10) 4 ½" squares
Cut (3) 3½" x WOF strips
Subcut (36) 3½" squares
Cut (2) 2" x WOF strips
Subcut (24) 2" squares

DARK AQUA (COLOR 3):
Cut one (1) 4½" x WOF strip
Subcut eight (8) 4½" squares
Cut three (3) 3½" x WOF strips
Subcut twenty-eight (28) 3½" squares
Cut three (3) 2" x WOF strips
Subcut forty-eight (48) 2" squares

FUCHSIA (COLOR 4):
Cut one (1) 4½" x WOF strip
Subcut six (6) 4½" squares

Cut three (3) 3½" x WOF strips
Subcut twenty (20) 3½" squares
Cut one (1) 3½" x WOF strip and set aside
for strip piecing

LIGHT AQUA (COLOR 5)
Cut one (1) 4½" x WOF strip
Subcut four (4) 4½" squares
Cut two (2) 3½" x WOF strips
Subcut twelve (12) 3½" squares
Cut two (2) 2" x WOF strips
Subcut twenty-four (24) 2" squares

DARK GREEN (COLOR 6)
Cut three (3) 3½" x WOF strips
Subcut thirty-six (36) 3½" squares
Cut one (1) 3½" x WOF strip and set aside
for strip piecing
Cut two (2) 2" x WOF strips and set aside for
strip piecing

BLACK (COLOR 7)
Cut seven (7) 2" x WOF strips
Subcut (144) 2" squares

LIGHT GREEN (COLOR 8)
Cut three (3) 4½" x WOF strips
Subcut twenty-four (24) 4½" squares

BINDING
Cut eleven (11) 2½" x WOF strips and set
aside

Assembly

Read through the entire instructions before you start assembly. There are four (4) different blocks in this quilt top, with varying color combinations. I will go over the basic instructions for each element in the blocks first, followed by instructions for the color placement for each block in the quilt.

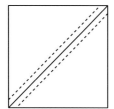

Fig. 1

HALF-SQUARE TRIANGLES WITH SMALL TRIANGLE

This explains the HST construction in the Cross blocks as well as the Diamond blocks.

1. Place a White 4½" square and a colored (shown as Grey) 4½" square right sides together.

2. Draw a diagonal line from corner to corner on the White fabric.

3. Sew the squares together with a line on both sides of the drawn line (fig. 1).

Fig. 2

4. Cut along the drawn line to get two (2) HST units and press seams toward the Dark fabric (fig. 2).

5. Trim HSTs to a 3½" x 3½" square (fig. 3).

Fig. 3

6. Place the colored (shown as black) 2" square right sides together in the corner of the White triangle of the HST unit. Draw a diagonal line from corner to corner.

Fig. 4

Fig. 5

7. Sew along the drawn line (fig. 4) then trim excess fabric, leaving a ¼" seam allowance and press seams (fig. 5).

FLYING GEESE SQUARES

These will be used for the Cross blocks only. Make thirty-six (36).

Fabric Cuts Needed to Make (36) Units

Thirty-six (36) Dark Green (color 6) 3½" squares

Seventy-two (72) Black (color 7) 2" squares

Seventy-two (72) White 2" x 3½" rectangles

1. Draw a diagonal line from corner to corner on the wrong side of each black 2" square.

2. Place a Black 2" square right sides together in the upper-left corner of a Dark Green 3½" square and sew along the drawn line (fig. 6).

3. Trim excess fabric, leaving a ¼" seam allowance and press seams (fig. 7).

4. Place a black 2" square right sides together in the upper-right corner of the Dark Green 3½" square and sew along the drawn line (fig. 8).

5. Trim excess fabric, leaving a ¼" seam allowance and press seams (fig. 9).

6. Place a White 2" x 3½" rectangle right sides together on both sides of the unit as shown in figure 10. Sew together using a ¼" seam allowance, then press seams out (fig. 11).

7 Two (2) HSTs with triangle units will be sewn together as shown (fig. 12) then sewn to a Flying Geese Square unit. There will be four (4) units like this with varying color combos in each of the nine (9) Cross blocks. Color and placement come later in the instructions.

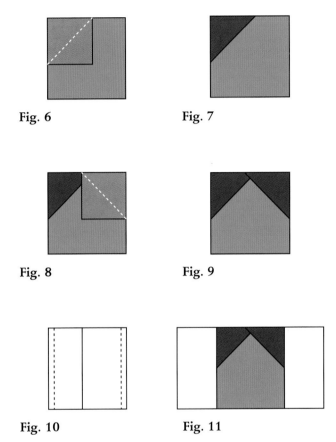

Fig. 6   **Fig. 7**

Fig. 8   **Fig. 9**

Fig. 10   **Fig. 11**

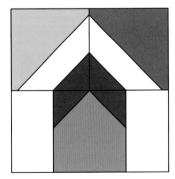

Fig. 12. Make 36.

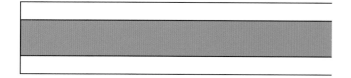

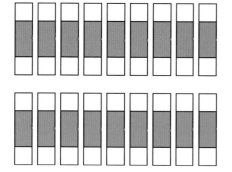

Fig. 13

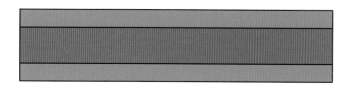

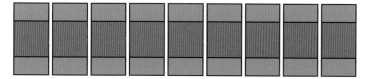

Fig. 14

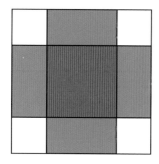

Fig. 15

STRIP PIECED NINE-PATCH UNITS

These will be used for the centers of the nine (9) Cross blocks.

Fabric Cuts Needed to Make (9) Units

Two (2) White 2" x WOF strips

One (1) Dark Green (color 6) 3½" x WOF strips

One (1) Fuchsia (color 4) 3½" x WOF strip

One (1) Dark Green (color 6) 2" x WOF strip

1. Sew the two (2) White 2" strips on both sides of the Dark Green (color 6) 3½" strip. Press seams toward the Green strip.

2. Subcut the strip at 2" to get eighteen (18) rectangles 2" x 6½" as shown in figure 13.

3. Sew the two (2) Dark Green (color 6) 2" strips on both sides of the Fuchsia (color 4) 3½" strip. Press seams toward the Green strips.

4. Subcut the strip at 3½" to get nine (9) rectangles 3½" x 6½" as shown in figure 14.

5. Sew two (2) White/Green 2" x 6½" rectangles to the top and bottom of one (1) Green/Fuchsia 3½" x 6½" rectangle. Press seams (fig. 15).

TRIANGLE SQUARES

These units come in two (2) sizes: 6½"
square for the Cross blocks which use the White
6½" square with a 3½" colored square; and a
3½" square for the Diamond blocks which use a
White 3½" square with a 2" colored square. The
instructions show how to make the unit and do
not include colors or sizes—that comes later.

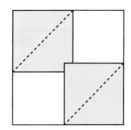
Fig. 16

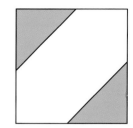
Fig. 17

1. Draw a diagonal line from corner to
corner on the wrong side of two (2) colored
small squares.

2. Place the squares right sides together
on opposite sides of the large White square and
sew along the drawn line (fig. 16).

3. Trim the excess fabric, leaving a ¼"
seam allowance and press seams toward the
darker fabric (fig. 17).

FILLER BLOCKS

There are two (2) versions of the Filler block.
I will show you how to piece these blocks
without the coloring (fig. 18).

These blocks will use the following cuts:
  White 6½" x 12½" rectangles
  White 3½" x 6½" rectangles
  White 6½" x 6½" squares
  (Colors 1, 2, 3, 4, 5) 3½" x 3½" squares
  (Colors 2, 3, 5) 2" x 2" squares

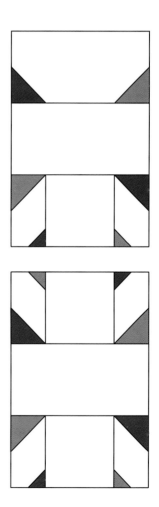
Fig. 18

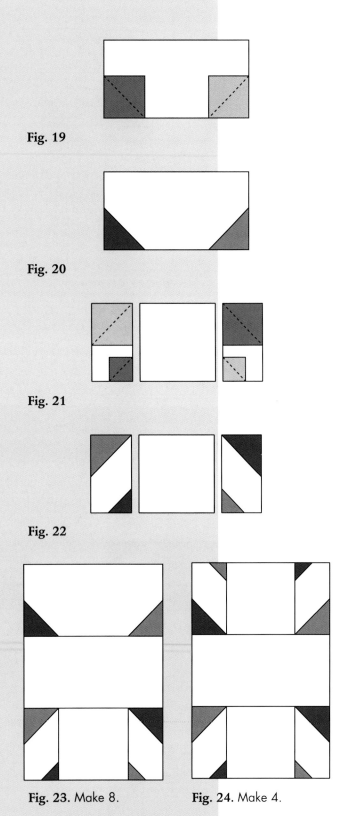

Fig. 19

Fig. 20

Fig. 21

Fig. 22

Fig. 23. Make 8.   **Fig. 24.** Make 4.

1. Place two (2) colored 3½" squares right sides together in each bottom corner of the White 6½" x 12½" rectangle. Draw a diagonal line from corner to corner on each 3½" square as shown in figure 19 and sew along the drawn line.

2. Trim the excess fabric leaving a ¼" seam allowance and press seams toward the Dark fabric. Set aside (fig. 20).

3. Draw a diagonal line on the wrong side of the 3½" squares and place right sides together at the **top** of a White 3½" x 6½" rectangle. Do this to two (2) rectangles for both sides of the unit. Use figure 21 for line placement.

4. Draw a diagonal line on the wrong side of the 2" squares and place right sides together at the **bottom** and opposite side of the White 3½" x 6½" rectangle. Do this to two (2) rectangles for both sides of the unit. Use figure 21 for line placement.

5. Sew along the drawn lines. Trim excess fabric leaving a ¼" seam allowance and press seams toward the Dark fabric (fig. 22).

6. Sew the two (2) rectangle units on opposite sides of a White 6½" x 6½" square as shown in figure 22. Press seams.

7. Sew together the two (2) rectangle units just made with a White 12½" x 6½" rectangle as shown in figure 23. There will be eight (8) blocks like this.

8. Sew together two (2) rectangle pieced units to a White 6½" x 12½" rectangle as shown in figure 24. Press seams. You will have four (4) blocks like this.

Fig. 25. Color code diagram

Fig. 26. Cross Block 1A. Make 3.

Fig. 27. Cross Block 2A. Make 4.

Fig. 28. Cross Block 3A. Make 2.

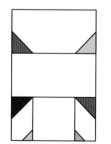

Fig. 29. Filler Block 4A. Make 2.

CROSS BLOCKS

You will need the following units to complete one (1) Cross block:

Eight (8) HSTs with small triangles
Four (4) Flying Geese squares
One (1) Strip-pieced Nine-Patch
Four (4) triangle squares

Sew the block like a Nine-Patch. Assemble three (3) units in each row, then sew them together. Press well.

Make three 3 (1A) blocks in this colorway using colors 1 (Dark Plum) and 2 (Light Plum) for the outside colors (fig. 26).

Make four (4) (2A) blocks in this colorway using colors 2 (Light Plum), 3 (Dark Aqua) and 4 (Fuchsia) for the outside colors (fig. 27).

Make two (2) (3A) blocks in this colorway using colors 1 (Dark Plum), 4 (Fuchsia), and 5 (Light Aqua) for the outside colors (fig. 28).

FILLER BLOCKS

Make two (2) Filler (4A) blocks in this colorway and placement (fig. 29) using the following color fabrics with White fabric per block:

One (1) Dark Plum (color 1) 3½" square triangle
Two (2) Light Plum (color 2) 3½" square triangles
One (1) DarkAqua (color 3) 3½" square triangle
One (1) Dark Aqua (color 3) 2" square triangle
One (1) Light Aqua (color 5) 2" square triangle

Make two (2) Filler (4B) blocks in this colorway and placement (fig. 30) using the following color fabrics with White fabric per block:

One (1) Dark Plum (color 1) 3½" square triangle

Two (2) Light Plum (color 2) 3½" square triangles

One (1) Light Aqua (color 3) 3½" square triangle

One (1) Dark Aqua (color 5) 2" square triangle

One (1) Light Aqua (color 3) 2" square triangle

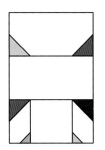

Fig. 30. Filler block 4B. Make 2.

Make (2) Filler (5A) blocks in this colorway and placement (fig. 31) using the following color fabrics with White fabric per block:

(1) Dark Aqua (color 5) 3½" square triangle

(2) Fuchsia (color 4) 3½" square triangles

(1) Light Aqua (color 3) 3½" square triangle

(1) Light Plum (color 2) 2" square triangle

(1) Light Aqua (color 3) 2" square triangle

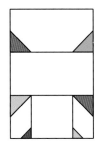

Fig. 31. Filler block 5A. Make 2.

Make (2) Filler (5B) blocks in this colorway and placement (fig. 32) using the following color fabrics with White fabric per block:

One (1) Light Aqua (color 3) 3½" square triangle

Two (2) Fuchsia (color 4) 3½" square triangles

One (1) Dark Aqua (color 5) 3½" square triangle

One (1) Light Aqua (color 3) 2" square triangle

One (1) Light Plum (color 2) 2" square triangle

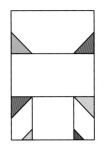

Fig. 32. Filler block 5A. Make 2.

Make (2) Filler (6A) blocks in this colorway and placement (fig. 33) using the following color fabrics with White fabric per block:

One (1) Dark Plum (color 1) 3½" square triangle

Two (2) Light Plum (color 2) 3½" square triangles

One (1) Light Aqua (color 3) 3½" square triangle

One (1) Light Plum (color 2) 2" square triangle

Two (2) Light Aqua (color 3) 2" square triangles

One (1) Dark Aqua (color 5) 2" square triangle

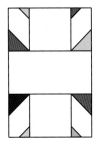

Fig. 33. Filler block 6A. Make 2.

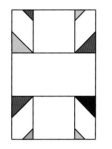

Fig. 34. Filler block 6B. Make 2.

Make (2) Filler (6B) blocks in this colorway and placement (fig. 34) using the following color fabrics with White fabric per block:

One (1) Dark Plum (color 1) 3½" square triangle
Two (2) Light Plum (color 2) 3½" square triangles
One (1) Light Aqua (color 3) 3½" square triangle
One (1) Light Plum (color 2) 2" square triangle
Two (2) Light Aqua (color 3) 2" square triangles
One (1) Dark Aqua (color 5) 2" square triangle

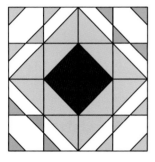

Fig. 35. Diamond block

Fig. 36

DIAMOND BLOCKS:

To make the Diamond blocks (fig. 35) you will need to have:

Eight (8) HSTs with small triangle
Four (4) HSTs (DarkPlum/LightGreen)
Four (4) triangle square units

All the directions on how to piece each element of the blocks have been covered, except for the HST without the small triangle. Just use the same directions found on (Page 100) to make a HST 3½" x 3½" square using the Dark Plum (color 1) and Light Green (color 8) 4½" squares (fig. 36).

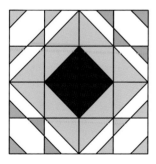

Fig. 37. Diamond block 7A. Make 2

Make (2) Diamond (7A) blocks (fig. 37). You will need the following:

Two (2) Light Aqua (color 3) triangle square units
Two (2) Dark Aqua (color 5) triangle square units
Four (4) HSTs with small triangles in colors 3 (Light Aqua), 8 (Light Green), and White
Four (4) HSTs with small triangles in colors 5 (Dark Aqua), 8 (Light Green), and White
Four (4) HST Dark Plum (color 1) and Light Green (color 8)

Make (2) Diamond (8A) blocks (fig. 38): you will need the following:

Two (2) Light Aqua (color 3) triangle square units

Two (2) Light Plum (color 2) triangle square units

Four (4) HSTs with small triangles in colors 3 (Light Aqua), 8 (Light Green), and White

Four (4) HSTs with small triangles in colors 2 (Light Plum), 8 (Light Green), and White

Four (4) HSTs in Dark Plum (color 1) and Light Green (color 8)

Sew the Diamond blocks together in rows then sew the rows together. Use a ¼" seam allowance and press seams well.

Fig. 38. Diamond block 8A. Make 2.

Final Assembly

Use figure 39 for block placement.

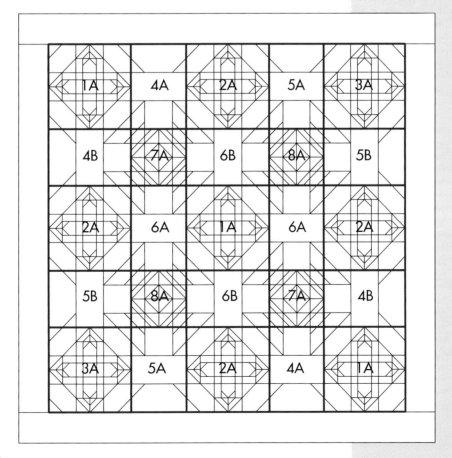

Fig. 39. Block placement

Sew the blocks into rows then sew the rows together.

Add borders for the final touch.

Sew the White 7" x 84" border strips to each side of the quilt. Trim excess fabric and press seams out.

Sew the White 7" x 96" border strips to the top and bottom of the quilt (fig. 40). Trim excess fabric and press seams out. Congrats on a job well done! Now for the real fun, the quilting!

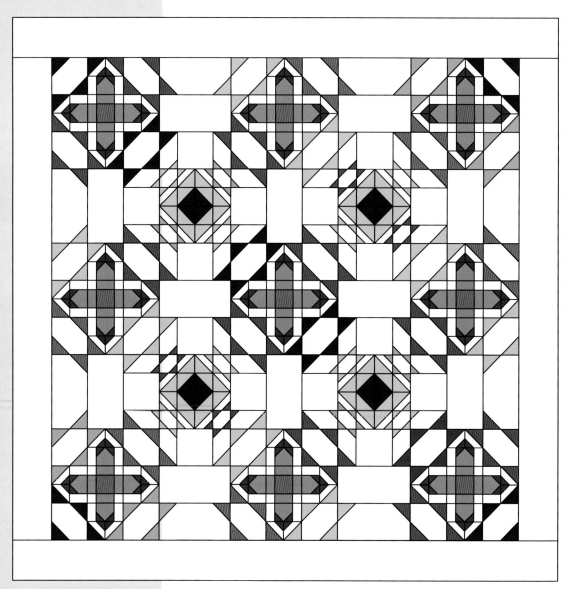

Fig. 40. Quilt top assembled

PLAYTIME – The Quilting!

PLAYTIME is my favorite design in this book, which is why it is the last project in the book—"last the best of all the game," right? Everything from the design, the piecing, and the quilting scream "secondary design," and this quilt turned out exactly as I wanted it to. Pictures can never do this quilt justice, but believe me—the design is amazing and the colors are perfect. PLAYTIME was really fun to quilt and not too difficult, so I hope that you enjoy quilting this design as much as I did.

There are four (4) fillers (figs. 41–44, p. 111) in this quilt top. Three (3) of these fillers are hopefully familiar designs for you, especially if you finished the previous projects in the book and have read my first book, *Quilting Wide Open Spaces*. The **Swirl-Pebble** (fig. 43) is a newer design but is simply a random Swirl with the occasional Pebble. You can do it! Free motion, baby!

The border is incorporated into the secondary design of the quilt blocks, so be aware of the line placement before you quilt

Fig. 41. Swirl

Fig. 42. Swirl 2

Fig. 43. Swirl-Pebble

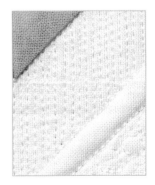

Fig. 44. Up and Down, Side to Side

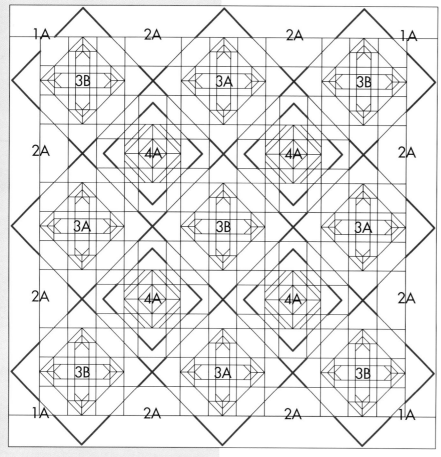

Fig. 45. Quilting designs outline and placement diagram

this top. The instructions will go through each section of the quilt, but the outline needs to be correct if this quilt design is going to work for you. You can pre-draw these lines if you feel more comfortable, but it is not necessary if you follow the outline (fig. 45).

In each section of the quilting you will need to stabilize the area that you are working on. It won't always be the stitch in the ditch, but the straight stitch outside the line of a design. Stabilizing will help to avoid puckers in your quilt top. There are four design sections in the quilt top. Use figure 45 for placement. Okay, here we go!

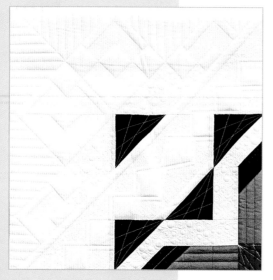

Fig. 46. Detail showing Section 1A quilting.

SECTION 1A (figs. 46 (below) and 47, p. 113)

1. Draw a diagonal center line for reference in the corner of the border strip as shown in Yellow. Draw a center line from the top of the Cross block to the outer edge of the quilt as shown in Yellow.

2. Draw the outside lines of the on-point square secondary design of the Cross block as shown in Neon Green.

Secondary **Designs** I Judi Madsen

3. Draw a 2" grid in the border of the quilt as shown in Neon Green.

4. In the middle row of squares in the grid, draw an X as shown in Pink. This will create the small on-point squares in the border design.

5. Draw the outside lines for the square motifs as shown in Purple referencing points 1, 2, 3, and 4.

6. Draw two (2) lines ½" from the outside lines to mimic the arrow shape in the square motif as shown in Blue.

7. Draw ½" spaced vertical and horizontal lines in the outside area of the border design as shown in the diagram in Light Green.

SECTION 2A (figs. 48 and 49)

The outside lines of the on-point squares should be drawn first, then the following:

1. Draw the vertical straight lines 2" apart as shown in Yellow/Green.

2. Draw the horizontal straight lines 2" apart as shown in Blue/Green.

3. Draw the center on-point main square as shown in Blue starting at point 1 connecting all the way to point 4 and back to point 1.

4. In the middle row of squares along the top of the design draw an X in each of the squares. Continue drawing X's in the center square rows of the Blue on-point square as shown in orange.

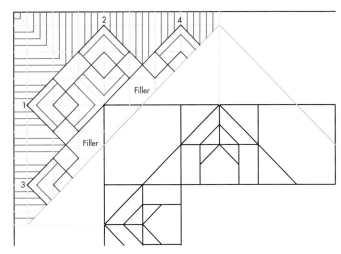

Fig. 47. Corner border quilting design diagram 1A. Diagram full size on the CD.

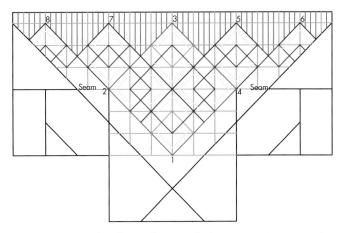

Fig. 48. Center border quilting path diagram 2A. Diagram full size on the CD.

Fig. 49. The drawing of 2A should be similar to the quilt in the photo.

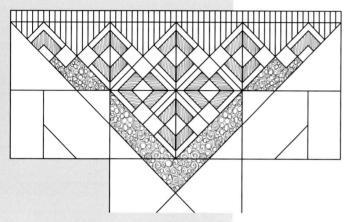

Fig. 50. Center Border Quilting Design diagram 2B. Diagram full size on the CD.

Fig. 51. Center Border Design detail

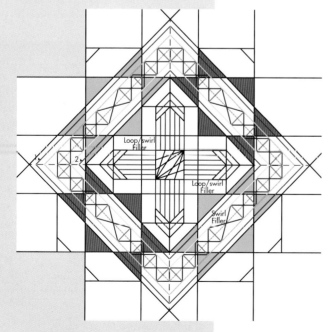

Fig. 52. Cross block quilting path diagram 3A. Diagram full size on the CD.

5. In the center of the large on-point square, draw an X connecting the other lines as shown in Purple.

6. Draw the remaining square motifs, shown in Maroon, making sure to be aware of the placement by referencing points 5, 6, 7, and 8.

7. Draw two (2) lines to mimic the arrow shape ½" away from the outside line of the square motif as shown in Yellow.

8. Draw ½" spaced vertical lines in the outside area of the border design as shown in the diagram.

QUILTING INSTRUCTIONS FOR 1A AND 2A

There is not a set quilting path for this quilt design. However, you will be traveling over previous lines to get from one area to the next.

1. Quilt the outside lines in the on-point squares.

2. Quilt the straight lines in the main design of the square motifs, outlining the center on-point square area, and then fill in the remaining lines of the design. In each square motif you will add detail inside the arrow shape with an up-and-down/side-to-side stitch as shown in figure 50.

3. Quilt the straight vertical lines on the outside edge of the design.

4. Free motion quilt a **swirl/pebble** filler in the remaining area of the design as shown in figure 50.

This is what it will look like (fig. 51, p. 114).

CROSS BLOCKS – SECTION 3A
(fig. 52, p. 114)

The outside lines of the on-point square should be drawn first. Use the quilting outline on p. 114 as a reference.

1. Draw ½" spaced lines in the Green fabric of the Cross block as shown in the diagram as Red.

2. Draw a line mimicking the arrow in the Black fabric in the center of the arrow as shown in the diagram as Orange.

3. The white area on the outside of the Cross block will be quilted with a **swirl/pebble** filler.

4. Draw four (4) lines to make a smaller on-point square ½" away from the outside lines of the block as shown in the diagram as line #1 in Red.

5. Draw four (4) lines to make a smaller on-point square ½" away from the inside lines of the block as shown in the diagram as line #2 in Red.

6. Draw four (4) lines to make another on-point square directly in the center of the two (2) lines drawn in steps 4 and 5, shown as a dotted line in the diagram as Orange.

7. Draw eight (8) lines to make two (2) on-point squares 1" away on both sides of the Orange dotted line as shown in the diagram as Yellow.

8. In the corners of each point of the square, draw two (2) lines to make a 2" square as shown in the diagram as Green.

9. Draw three (3) lines out 2" from the Green lines drawn previously to make three (3) more 2" squares as shown in the diagram as Blue. In each center area of the block you will have a rectangle.

10. Draw lines, making an X in each square and rectangle in the block as shown in the diagram as Purple. The corner squares will not have an X, but will be two (2) squares as shown in the diagram (fig. 52, p. 114).

11. The Purple lines will be quilted; the remaining negative space will be filled with a free motion **Swirl**.

Fig. 53. Cross block quilting detail

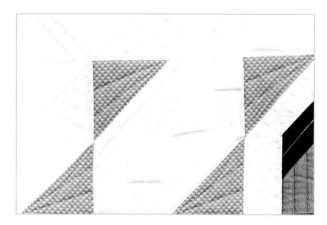

Fig. 54. Triangles

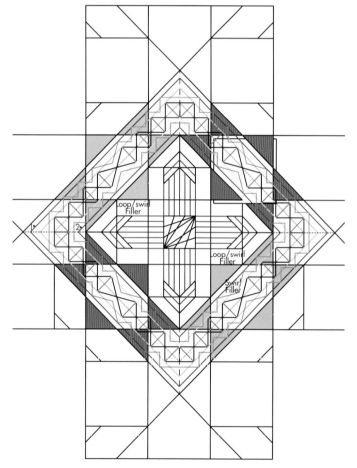

Fig. 55. Cross block quilting path diagram 3B. Diagram full size on the CD.

QUILTING 3A

1. Stabilize and quilt the cross first, then fill in around the cross piecing.

2. Stitch in the ditch around the triangles and stitch each area of the block as you move across the top of the quilt (fig. 54). There really isn't a right or wrong quilting path, just stabilize as you go.

The triangles were stitched with simple lines for balanced quilting. The reference points are at each 1" along the 90° angle of the triangle.

The directions for drawing and quilting 3B are the same directions for 3A except that there is one more step in the drawing. You need to add a border ¼" away from the lines of the center squares of the design. Use figure 55 and the photo in figure 53, page 115, for reference.

DIAMOND BLOCKS SECTION 4A
(fig. 56, p. 117)

The outside lines of the on-point square should be drawn first. Use the quilting outline on p. 117 as a reference.

1. Draw ½" spaced lines in the Purple center on-point square as shown in the diagram as Yellow.

2. Draw ½" spaced lines to make two (2) smaller on-point squares inside the Green fabric as shown in the diagram as Yellow.

Fig. 56. Diamond block quilting path diagram 4A.
Diagram full size on the CD.

3. Free motion quilt **Swirl** in between the lines in the Green fabric.

4. Draw lines to complete the on-point square shapes inside the design shown in the diagram as lines 1 and 2 in Red.

5. Draw lines to make an on-point square ¼" smaller than the square next to it as shown in the diagram as lines 3, 4, and 5 in Green. The inside area of line 5 will be filled with an up-and-down/side-to side-stitch.

6. Draw lines to make two (2) on-point squares ½" away and inside lines 3 and 4 as shown in the diagram as lines 6 and 7 in Yellow.

7. Draw vertical and horizontal ½" spaced lines between lines 6 and 7 as shown in the diagram as Blue, starting in the center point of the section.

8. Between lines 4 and 2, draw an on-point square directly in the center of the two (2) lines.

Fig. 57. Diamond block quilting detail

Fig. 58. PLAYTIME on the longarm

9. Draw eight (8) lines to make two (2) on-point squares ½" away on both sides of the line drawn in step 8.

10. In the corners of each point of the square, draw two (2) lines to make a 1" square as shown as Red in the diagram.

11. Draw five (5) lines out 1" from the Red lines drawn previously to make five (5) more 1" squares as shown as Yellow in the diagram. In each center area of the block you will have a rectangle.

12. Draw lines, making an X in each square and rectangle in the block as shown in the diagram as Pink. The corner squares will not have an X, but will be two squares as shown in the diagram.

13. The Pink lines will be quilted and the remaining negative space will be filled with a free-motion **Swirl-Pebble**.

QUILTING DIAMOND BLOCK 4A

As with all the sections in this quilt top, you will quilt as you go, stabilizing by stitching in the ditch or by stitching the outside straight lines of the on-point squares. Notice in my own quilting picture that I work on the areas that fit in the throat space of my machine.

Congrats on a job well done! Doesn't it feel great to finish?

About the Author

Judi is an award-winning quilter, author, and instructor. She has traveled the world teaching to bring the joy of quilting to others throughout the USA, Canada, Australia, and Norway. She started her own pattern line when she was 25 and has self-published over 50 different designs for her company Green Fairy Quilts. Her first book, *Quilting Wide Open Spaces*, was published by AQS in 2013. She has an online class with iquilt.com called "Quilting Makes a Difference" where she teaches about two different takes on quilting, modern and traditional. She loves being able to share her passion about quilting with others in the hopes to inspire them on their own quilting journey.

Judi is married to her high school sweetheart, Clint, and they have four children. Together they own www.greenfairyquilts.com, an online business that started by selling Judi's pattern but has expanded to fabric and notions as well. They live in beautiful Saint George, Utah.

Enjoy these and more from AQS

AQS Publishing brings the latest in quilt topics to satisfy the traditional to modern quilter. Interesting techniques, vivid color, and clear directions make these books your one-stop for quilt design and instruction. With its leading Quilt-Fiction series, mystery, relationship, and community all merge as stories are pieced together to keep you spellbound.

Whether Quilt-Instruction or Quilt-Fiction, pick one up from AQS today.

#12536

#12510

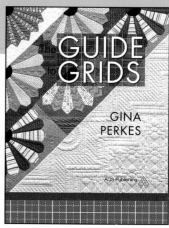

#12526

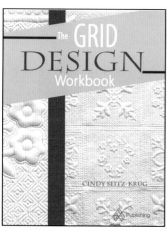

#12532

#12512

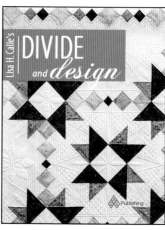

#10274

#12518

#12514

#12534

AQS publications are available nationwide. Call or visit AQS

1-800-626-5420
www.shopAQS.com